Praise for
Inward Revolution

"This book could only have been written by a ministry professional with a robust prayer life, irrefutable command of scripture, and radical theological vision for the Church. Lawrence Rodgers challenges us to honor God, self, and community by sitting in the presence of God to listen to a speaking God who is alive and active in the world—a revealed God in the person of Jesus Christ who modeled a disciplined prayer life. Part autobiographical, part Bible study, part spiritual practicum, *Inward Revolution* is a reader-friendly gift to the Church that asks its readers to meet God not only in the pulpit or on the pew but in the prayer closet to hear what an all-wise, loving, gracious, and merciful God will say to us."
   —**Kenyatta R. Gilbert,** Dean and Professor of Homiletics,
   Howard University School of Divinity

"If you desire to delve deeper and expand your own personal spiritual journey, *Inward Revolution* is a must-read. Dr. Rodgers masterfully guides and challenges the reader into a greater spiritual awakening through spiritual practices. His vulnerability in sharing stories is compelling. The 'beloved community' is invited to embrace the power of *faith and conviction* that leads to confession and *forgiveness*—and ultimately to personal and communal *transformation*. I recommend this book to seekers and disciples willing to acquire a fuller arsenal of spiritual disciplines that enable them to live and thrive, experiencing Christ's complete joy."
   —**Rev. Nikita McCalister,** MBA, MDiv, President,
   American Baptist Churches USA

"Lawrence Rodgers's wonderful book pursues a question most of us have asked: Where am I now, and where do I want to be? Written in inviting prose and assisted by reflections on our current political and social landscape, Rodgers offers his readers an opportunity to reevaluate Jesus's wisdom for living; he gives us an empathetic and refreshing counterargument against spiritual malaise."
   —**Arthur Sutherland,** Associate Professor of Theology,
   Loyola University Maryland

"Character. That's what this book is about. And that's where this book originates. *Inward Revolution* is a volume birthed by a pastor who knows and cares for human beings. Pastor Lawrence Rodgers's accessible work transcends the typical volume on spiritual formation because it begins with 'the sound of the genuine,' which is the person of Lawrence Rodgers, who is living out the realities he advocates and loves and is concerned enough for his reading flock that he invites us to join him on the journey. *Inward Revolution* is practical advice from a trusted minister who, through his seasoned and kind wisdom, shows a pathway to healthy and fruitful living. I highly recommend the book, in part because it affords readers the opportunity to 'sit across the table' from a very good man!"

—**David Fleer,** Retired Professor of Homiletics, Lipscomb University

"Pastor Lawrence Rodgers's *Inward Revolution* is a vital testimony that true contentment requires that we engage with our internal voice, each other, and the divine. To do this means training, just as an athlete works out to succeed. Because of years of academic training, pastoral leadership, and personal spiritual development, Rev. Lawrence has much to share about the process. He invites you to participate in an inward revolution that promises profound results, providing a practical guide to the journey."

—**Alice Ogden Bellis,** Professor of Hebrew Bible, Howard University School of Divinity

"Pastor Rodgers's *Inward Revolution* is a masterclass in doing the difficult inner soul work prior to leading souls to salvation. This work is akin to flight attendants' instructions of putting on your mask before assisting others with theirs. He makes the case for contemplative practices with wonderful strategies that allow us to be still and listen for God's voice. This work is a must-read for pastoral leaders."

—**Dr Tanya Brice,** Provost and Vice President of Academic Affairs, Saint Martin's University, Lacey, Washington

"Pastor Lawrence Rodgers is a socially conscious activist. So when I saw that he was writing a book on spirituality, I was intrigued. But in leafing through its pages, I discovered the Source of his vision. Like

Howard Thurman, Richard Rohr, Barbara Holmes, and other contemplative activists, Pastor Rodgers identifies the resources of interiority that sustain vision and practice. In an age where activism and spirituality remain bifurcated and polarized, this text gives insight to the spiritual depths that anchor the soul and become the launching pad for personal, communal, and social change. I'm definitely adding this book to my syllabi at Pastor Rodgers's alma mater: Howard University School of Divinity."
—**Dr. Harold Dean Trulear,** President of Healing Communities, Professor of Applied Theology, Howard University School of Divinity

"Before standing in front of the people of God to proclaim the Word of God with the power of the Spirit of God, pastors must survive the crucible of unrelenting pressure, insatiable demands, and impossible expectations they encounter as shepherds of the church of God. Those who prioritize the cultivation of their spiritual lives survive the crucible of pastoral ministry. It is they who leave an enduring spiritual mark upon those they serve. The apostolic wisdom places the preacher's spiritual life before their public ministry. Lawrence Rodgers stands in the long, rich, and storied line of pastors and theologians who turn first to the care of their own souls before venturing to care for the souls of others. This engaging book briefly sketches his spiritual journey from childhood to his presence in one of the most storied pulpits in America. He shares generously of the lessons he's learned about the spiritual nurture and self-care that prepare a pastor to proclaim and prove the life-changing power of the gospel of Jesus Christ. Take a moment to linger over this book. Refresh your soul. Return to your first love. Pastor Rodgers will walk with you for a bit. Hear him."
—**Bud Brown,** Turnaround Pastors

"*Inward Revolution* is a cultural and theological counternarrative that wrestles with the timeless question, 'How you gonna win when you ain't right within?' Lawrence Rodgers has composed a poignant and relevant account of his own archaeological revelations of his soul. A must-read."
—**Rev. Erica Williams Scott,** Founder, Set It Off Movement

"This book is a must-read for anyone who is serious about reaping the benefits of spiritual discipline. Specifically, we are shown the accomplishments that follow the kind of actions, attitudes, and behaviors Jesus Christ taught and exemplified. I truly enjoyed Pastor Rodgers's biblical insight, literary applications, organic analysis, and experiential perception. It was a meaningful book that although true to mainstream Baptist doctrine, is helpful for people of varying religious or nonreligious backgrounds. *Inward Revolution* adheres to the highest academic and ethical standards and still is accessible to folks of a multiplicity of educational achievement. Every time I read it, I see something new. It is a gift that will continue to give, and if put into practice, you will achieve its mantra!"

—**Charles Christian Adams,** Senior Pastor, Hartford Memorial Baptist Church, Detroit; President, Michigan Progressive Baptist Convention; 1st Vice President, Midwest Region of Progressive National Baptist Convention Inc.

"Pastor Lawrence Rogers embarked on a rigorous season of introspection as the Lord called him to lead the church he pastors into renewal and revitalization. His quest involved more strength and skill than he could begin to imagine. In *Inward Revolution*, Pastor Rogers chronicles his own spiritual journey of radical transformation by applying simple spiritual disciplines to fuel a spiritual revolution in his life. I invite you to join him in this engaging journey to grow deeper in your walk with the Savior so you might better serve others. You will be glad you did!"

—**Dr. Gordon Penfold,** Turnaround Pastors

"Rodgers's work is an important contribution. One can only hope for more from this gifted theologian and pastor."

—**Dr. William Dahaner,** cofounder of Institute of Pastoral Studies and Pastor of Christ Church Cranbrook

INWARD REVOLUTION

A JOURNEY OF RADICAL TRANSFORMATION

LAWRENCE W. RODGERS

LEAFWOOD
PUBLISHERS
an imprint of Abilene Christian University Press

INWARD REVOLUTION
A Journey of Radical Transformation

LEAFWOOD
P U B L I S H E R S
an imprint of Abilene Christian University Press

Copyright © 2024 by Lawrence W. Rodgers

ISBN 978-1-68426-431-5 | LCCN 2023049737

Printed in the United States of America

ALL RIGHTS RESERVED | No part of this publication may be reproduced, stored in a retrieval system, or transmitted in any form by any means—electronic, mechanical, photocopying, recording, or otherwise—without prior written consent.

All Scripture quotations, unless otherwise noted, are taken from the New Revised Standard Version Bible. Copyright © 1989, the Division of Christian Education of the National Council of the Churches of Christ in the United States of America. Used by permission. All rights reserved.

Scripture quotations noted AMPC are from the Amplified® Bible Classic Edition. Copyright © 1965, 1987 by The Lockman Foundation. Used by permission.

Scripture quotations noted CSB are from the Christian Standard Bible®. Copyright © 2017 by Holman Bible Publishers. Used by permission. Christian Standard Bible®, and CSB® are federally registered trademarks of Holman Bible Publishers.

Scripture quotations noted ESV are from The Holy Bible, English Standard Version®. Copyright © 2001 by Crossway, a publishing ministry of Good News Publishers. ESV® Text Edition: 2016. The ESV® text has been reproduced in cooperation with and by permission of Good News Publishers. Unauthorized reproduction of this publication is prohibited. All rights reserved.

Scripture quotations noted GNT are from the Good News Bible. © 1994 published by the Bible Societies/HarperCollins Publishers Ltd UK, Good News Bible. © American Bible Society 1966, 1971, 1976, 1992. Used with permission.

Scripture quotations noted KJV are taken from the King James Version of the Bible.

Scripture quotations noted KJ21 are taken from the 21st Century King James Version®. Copyright © 1994. Used by permission of Deuel Enterprises, Inc., Gary, SD 57237. All rights reserved.

Scripture quotations noted NABRE are taken from the New American Bible, revised edition. © 2010, 1991, 1986, 1970 Confraternity of Christian Doctrine, Washington, DC, and are used by permission of the copyright owner. All rights reserved.

Scripture quotations noted NCB are taken from the SAINT JOSEPH NEW CATHOLIC BIBLE®. Copyright © 2019 by Catholic Book Publishing Corp. Used with permission. All rights reserved.

Scripture quotations noted NIV are taken from the Holy Bible, New International Version®, NIV®. Copyright © 1973, 1978, 1984, 2011 by Biblica, Inc.™ Used by permission of Zondervan. All rights reserved worldwide.

Scripture quotations noted NKJV are taken from the New King James Version®. Copyright © 1982 by Thomas Nelson. Used by permission. All rights reserved.

Scripture quotations noted NLT are taken from the Holy Bible, New Living Translation. Copyright © 1996, 2004, 2007, 2015 by Tyndale House Foundation. Used by permission of Tyndale House Publishers, Inc., Carol Stream, IL 60188. All rights reserved.

LIBRARY OF CONGRESS CATALOGING-IN-PUBLICATION DATA
Names: Rodgers, Lawrence W., author.
Title: Inward revolution / Pastor Lawrence W. Rodgers.
Description: Abilene, Texas : Leafwood Publishers, [2024]
Identifiers: LCCN 2023049737 | ISBN 9781684264315 | ISBN 9781684269372 (ebook)
Subjects: LCSH: Fasting—Religious aspects—Christianity.
Classification: LCC BV5055 .R624 2024 | DDC 248.4/7—dc23/eng/20240315
LC record available at https://lccn.loc.gov/2023049737

Cover design by Greg Jackson, Thinkpen Design
Interior text design by Sandy Armstrong, Strong Design

Leafwood Publishers is an imprint of Abilene Christian University Press.
ACU Box 29138 | Abilene, Texas 79699

1-877-816-4455 | www.leafwoodpublishers.com

24 25 26 27 28 29 30 / 7 6 5 4 3 2 1

*This book is dedicated to my beautiful wife,
who has been a profound source of encouragement
throughout the writing of this volume, and to our three
wonderful children, who continually inspire me.*

CONTENTS

Foreword ·····13
Preface ·····17

INWARD REVOLUTION

1 Discernment ·····23
2 The Spiritual Recipe: Prayer, Fasting, and Study ·····43
3 Accepting Contentment ·····65
4 Community ·····77
5 Faith and Conviction ·····95
6 Transformation ·····111
7 Forgiveness ·····127

PRACTICUM

8 Spiritual Disciplines: A Practical Guide ·····141
9 Practical Keys to Meditation ·····151
10 The Practice of Simplicity ·····157

A Message to the Reader ·····165
Acknowledgments ·····167
About the Author ·····171

FOREWORD

The sound of the genuine is flowing through you. Don't be deceived and thrown off by all the noises that are part even of your dreams and your ambitions when you don't hear the sound of the genuine in you. Because that is the only true guide you will ever have and if you don't have that you don't have a thing. . . . Cultivate the discipline of listening to the sound of the genuine in yourself.[1]

Our world is deeply in need of spiritual practices. In this joyous book, a minister and scholar takes us on an inspiring journey, through the tumult of life, and into the divine mystery that is ever at the heart of faith. The traffic of our days crowds in upon us, the vastness of it all scatters us far and wide, and much gets buried and neglected within us. *Inward Revolution* is an invitation to divine rediscovery, a call to remember that under the many layers of our restless and uncertain lives there is, at our utmost center, an inward sea, a blissful stirring still.

I first met Lawrence Rodgers ten years ago, when he enrolled at Howard University School of Divinity, and where I served at the time as dean. As a graduate student, pastor, and family man, he was profoundly committed to exploring the interplay between the life of the mind and the life of the spirit, to grounding the just demands of faith in genuine liberative religious practice. Through the years, the sound of the genuine is resonant in Lawrence Rodgers's own life. His encounters with God and his illuminating grasp of the human condition in light of those sacred encounters have grounded and deepened his commitment to the people of God everywhere.

Inward Revolution is a compact tome and substantial testimony. Page by page, chapter by chapter, we journey with the author through techniques of spiritual discipline and contemplative practices and out into the daily walk of life. The litany of biblical, theological, and ethical reflections shared in these pages are filled with pastoral wisdom and delicate grace. From Howard Thurman and Harry Sawyerr to Barbara A. Holmes and Cole Arthur Riley, and countless more voices besides (the great ancestral and communal "cloud of witnesses" [Heb. 12:1]), the through line to vast reservoirs of the spirit—resources of inheritance, family, and faith—provide assurance and nourishment to the hunger of the human heart. Lawrence Rodgers shares a message of genuine and authentic spirituality for the healing of the nations and wounded lives in our day and time. His writing bears witness with a resplendent hope to God's dream for our humanity. The Spirit is present and working in our midst. God is with us. Beloved community awaits.

Alton B. Pollard III

President Emeritus, Louisville Presbyterian Theological Seminary
James and Marilyn Dunn Chair in Baptist Studies and University Professor of African American Studies, Wake Forest University

Note

[1] Howard Thurman, "The Sound of the Genuine," ed. Jo Moore Stewart, *Spelman Messenger* 96, no. 4 (Summer 1980): 14–15.

PREFACE

This book is a result of my spiritual and ministerial journeys to date, each of which involved much prayer and study and many challenges. We face a series of stimuli throughout life—objects and actions that prompt reactions. How we respond to those stimuli sets the trajectory of our journeys. We cannot control most of what occurs in our respective spheres, but we can control our reactions, and those should be heavenly influenced. In fact, when we make it a habit to always look above, to bring Jesus into our every thought, decision, and action, and to give our lives over to the Almighty, our reactions and responses to the stimuli of this world will be blessed.

For this reason, it is vital that we are intentional about self-edification and our spiritual growth. Theologian and modern-day philosopher Howard Thurman said it best in 1980—one year before his death—while delivering a baccalaureate address at Spelman College, a historically Black college and women's institution in Atlanta, Georgia:

> There is in every person something that waits and listens for the sound of the genuine in herself.... There is in you something that waits and listens for the sound of the genuine in yourself. Nobody like you has ever been born and no one like you will ever be born again—you are the only one. And if you miss the sound of the genuine in you, you will be [hindered] all the rest of your life. Because you will never be able to get a scent on who you are.
>
> Do you remember in the book Jesus and his disciples were going through the hills and there appeared in the turn of the road a man who was possessed of devils as they thought. In the full moon when the great tidal waves of energy swept through his organism and he became as ten men . . . screaming through the hills like an animal in pain and then he met Jesus on the road. And Jesus asked him one question: "Who are you; what's your name?" and for a moment his tilted mind righted itself and he said, "That's it, I don't know, there are legions of me. And they riot in my streets. If I only knew, then I would be whole."[1]

Sadly, too many people have no idea who they are, and because of that, many of those who don't know who they are run wild. Getting to know our true selves gives us the ability to control how we respond to a variety of circumstances. However, we cannot truly know ourselves without knowing our creator, who is God. So a part of getting to know ourselves is getting to know God, because the best of us is aligned with God's will, and the worst of us is not. To have the right response or the righteous response to the ups and downs of life means we must know our creator and how the creator would want us to respond.

We all know that inward transformation begins with "the man in the mirror," to quote Michael Jackson's famous song. He continues, "If you want to make the world a better place, take a look at yourself and then make a change."[2] It sounds so easy. Step one: just look at yourself; step two: make a change. What could be simpler?

This small book is an effort to help you do the hard work of spiritual transformation. It's an invitation to join me on the inward revolution journey. The volume is divided into two sections. The first delves both reflectively and theoretically into what the inward journey is, and it offers insights into topics that many people either avoid or find intimidating.

You will find that I emphasize the importance of study. Not just the study of Scripture, but also the study of ourselves, each other, creation, and the world at large. A lack of understanding often underlies our disagreements and conflicts; by committing to continuous learning, we can foster understanding and potentially increase harmony in our lives.

The first section offers other rewards as well. It explores the challenge of learning to be content but not complacent, and it explores the power you can find in loving a community as you would love yourself. We'll also discuss the importance of courageously acting upon your faith.

What is the fruit of a transformed life? What is the most telling sign that someone has truly undergone an inward revolution? It is their ability to forgive. The first section concludes with an exploration of forgiveness, examining the challenges we face when we struggle to either repent or forgive. The power to let go of grudges and bitterness is the ultimate sign of transformation.

The second section of this volume is a practicum, which offers hands-on ways to implement spiritual disciplines on your journey to the inward revolution. This section addresses the nitty-gritty details: how exactly to practice spiritual disciplines, how to incorporate meditation into a busy schedule, and how to lead a simple, content life without unnecessary anxiety over what you don't have while remaining grateful for what you do possess.

I genuinely hope this volume enriches your life as much as it has enriched mine in the writing and living of it. Welcome to the revolution: the inward revolution!

Notes

[1] Howard Thurman, "The Sound of the Genuine (Baccalaureate ceremony) (Spelman College), 1980 May 4," The Howard Thurman Digital Archive, https://thurman.pitts.emory.edu/items/show/838.

[2] Michael Jackson, "Man in the Mirror," track 4 on *Bad*, Westlake, 1987.

INWARD REVOLUTION

DISCERNMENT

When Jesus left Judea to return to Galilee, he passed through Samaria, where he met the woman at the well and revealed himself as the Messiah. The Samaritans and the Jews had their differences, yet despite those differences, the woman recognized that Jesus was indeed the Messiah, and she returned to her town to spread the good news. It is clear from this account in the Gospel of John that Jesus stopped in Samaria for the express purpose of casting a wide net, spreading his ministry beyond the Jewish nations.

We are called to do the same, just as Jesus instructed his first disciples. If we wish to spiritually grow, as Jesus instructed, we must first pray about and practice discernment. That is, we must make time to improve our spiritual life, which requires listening, observing, and becoming more self-aware, grateful, and kind. Throughout this book, we will unpack spiritual disciplines to assist us with our spiritual journey.

Everything we do is meant to glorify God, so it is imperative that we approach our relationships, our vocations, and even our leisure with a sense of purpose. No matter where we start, we should end somewhere else, physically and metaphorically. Otherwise, we are meandering, wasting God's precious gifts of time and talent.

Progress is a blessing from our good and great God, guiding us from points A to B and from B to C to D, and so on. Life is interesting, though, because we believers lean on God to help us reach our destination, and then we forget that our journey is not over. We get to point B and begin to listen less. By the time we reach points C and D, we have either decided we no longer need to listen or we simply fall out of habit.

Experience is a humbling teacher. As we go through life, we come to understand that we had better listen. At this fork in the road, I find that most take one of two paths. There are those who learn to listen and gain wisdom and those who learn the hard way, through the school of hard knocks. Sometimes, God gives us the same lesson over and over until we learn from it, until we become wiser.

God is so kind and generous to have placed wisdom all around us. We just need to be ever mindful of and open to God's presence. Wisdom personified cries out to us, asking how long the foolish will hate knowledge and the simple ones will love being simple (Prov. 1:20–22). The Bible says that wisdom is crying out for those who are listening, even crying for those who have gone before us. Wisdom cries out from the Word of God and from our experiences. We had better listen. We miss so much when we don't.

I remember a lesson I learned about listening. During my formative years, I had an opportunity to spend a day with two scholars, a theologian and a philosopher, each of whom I respected deeply. We were attending a Racial Unity Leadership Summit in Abilene, Texas. I had traveled the country attending these types of summits, where people of all backgrounds and churches gathered to discuss ways to break down walls of division and bring society together. The effort was led by Jerry Taylor, the director of the Carl Spain Center on Race Studies & Spiritual Action.

I was eager to learn from these two older gentlemen whom I had come to know and admire over several years. I considered them mentors and had the utmost respect for their academic journeys. The theologian was a Karl Barth and James Cone scholar. The philosopher was a Howard Thurman scholar. I was confident they could help me form my educational path. We spent the entire day together, and we had wonderful conversations. I interjected things here and there, and a few times I shared my thoughts and opinions. It was a lovely time and good fellowship. That night, however, I started to regret some of the words I said. Not because they were wrong. They were good words, but every time I spoke, I was declining the opportunity to listen more to what my companions were saying.

We must be willing to listen to those who went before us. There's an African proverb that says, "When an old person dies, a library burns to the ground." People are walking bodies of wisdom and information. We must spend time listening to them if we want to learn from their wisdom. God tells us, "Honor your father and your mother, so that your days may be long in the land that the LORD your God is giving you" (Exod. 20:12).

This is a valid statement. Why will our days be long? Because we have received the wisdom of those who have gone before us. We cannot receive this wisdom, however, if we're not willing to listen. As we listen, we learn. A lot of people believe, erroneously, that education is something that happens exclusively in a classroom, but learning happens everywhere, and many of the lessons are free. When we find ourselves in the midst of elders, those who have lived through good times and bad, we have an opportunity not only to listen, but also to learn from their mistakes, their insights, and their actions.

Many times, we miss out because we are not willing to listen. We must listen. Are we listening? God is sending messages our way all the time, through the wisdom of elders and also through the idealism of the young. Even after Jesus had cleansed the temple and cured the blind and the lame, the chief priests and scribes became angry as they heard the children crying out "Hosanna" (Matt. 21:9). The children didn't worry about power or tradition or culture. They saw Jesus plainly: "Hosanna to the Son of David!" So, they cried it out, praising Jesus. If those high priests and scribes, with all their haughtiness, had listened to the children, they would have been blessed. We must listen. Are we listening? The messages God sends are all around us. We must not neglect strangers and must show them hospitality, as some could be angels that we do not recognize (Heb. 13:2).

Even strangers can bless us. My 2017 trip to Ghana comes to mind. Two Howard University classmates, Vince Vann and Benjamin Mattocks, and I decided to make the trek upon graduation, so we fundraised to pay for it. Our goal was to have a culturally enriching experience, and we did. It was a meaningful trip. Instead of staying at hotels, we lodged with people in villages. I can never forget one particular host who fed us from her garden. Each day, we enjoyed freshly caught fish, vegetables, sugarcane, plantains, and more. She and her daughter were so kind that I felt guilty about it, undeserving. She had to remind me and my friends to remain comfortable and accept her hospitality. I learned that not accepting someone's gift is not only rude, but it also blocks their grace. We receive grace through acts of kindness toward others. I had to humble myself to receive so much hospitality from this beautiful person.

Consider the story of the woman at the well who proclaimed the message of God to the lost in John 4. She went to the well and listened to Jesus, and because she listened, she knew he was special. She left Jesus, went back to her village, and then returned to Jesus with many people. Think about a time when you were so excited about an event or a chance meeting that you wanted to share the experience with others. There's no greater gift than the good news of Jesus. We should have the same kind of excitement as the woman at the well, enthusiastically sharing the good news of Christ. Our excitement should garner attention, and rightfully so.

It was when Jesus had learned that the Pharisees had heard of the baptisms carried out by his disciples that he then left Judea and started back to Galilee (John 4:1–4). If you look at a map, you will see that Jesus did not have to go through Samaria to get to Galilee from Judea. He stopped there because he had something to do in Samaria. As he came to Sychar, a Samarian city, he rested by a well as the disciples traveled into the city to buy more food. It was at the well where he met a Samaritan woman coming to draw water, and he asked her to do the same for him (John 4:5–8).

It is important that we understand the significance of their conversation. For Jesus to ask this woman to give him a drink was scandalous at that time because he was a man and she was a woman, they were alone, and he was talking to her in the middle of the day, when most men were at work. In first-century culture, some viewed men as better than women, and it was taboo for men to speak to women in the middle of the day. Much of Jesus's ministry was spent ministering to women in an effort to reverse the cultural prejudices against femininity and women. Men had been allowed to divorce their wives for any reason, leaving women without the means to provide for themselves. Jesus was establishing protection for women when he proclaimed that any man who divorces his wife makes her a victim of adultery. In Matthew 5, we see Jesus discussing the problems of divorce—he was establishing protection for women against men who might marry a woman, have children with her, build a life with her, and then leave her for a younger woman when they were both middle-aged. He implores people to keep their oaths: "But I tell you, do not swear an oath at all: either by heaven, for it is God's throne; or by the earth, for it is his footstool; or by Jerusalem, for it is the city of the Great King" (Matt. 5:34–35 NIV).

Jesus further warns men about emotional infidelity, instructing that anyone who looks at a Victoria's Secret catalog lustfully has already committed adultery with that model in his heart. Of course, I am providing a modern-day example to bring to life the words of Matthew 5:28–29, where Jesus also tells them that if their right eye should cause them to sin, then they should gouge it out because it is better to lose one part of the body rather than the rest be thrown into Gehenna. The dangers of lust are that serious. Lust is a perversion, the exact opposite of love. Lust is self-seeking, where love is self-giving. Jesus is instructing men to love rightly, to avoid the temptation of lust. He again is offering protection for women, who at that time were considered to be at fault if men lusted after them. That mentality—women being blamed for crimes committed against them—still exists today. Imagine being a woman in that culture two thousand years ago. How liberating would Jesus's words have felt? When Jesus met the woman at the well, he saw her as a daughter and conscripted her to be an evangelist.

She enthusiastically went back to her village to spread the good news, and then she brought people to meet Jesus.

Because the woman at the well was considered beneath him, as the disciples demonstrated in John 4:27, people would naturally think there was only one thing a strange man could want by conversing with her, and that was something carnal, not spiritual. It was also likely taboo for the two to speak because the woman was a Samaritan. Some Judeans of the time looked down upon Samaritans. The Samaritan woman likely knew it was strange for Jesus to speak to her, yet she recognized that something out of the ordinary was happening. She then asked him how he, a Jew, would ask such a thing of a woman of Samaria (John 4:9). She knew this was not culturally acceptable. This was not to say that such androcentrism was exclusive to Judeans and their culture; the truth is, such male-dominated norms were a general part of the ancient Near Eastern culture during that time. Nevertheless, what I like about her is that she didn't allow ethnocentric mores to shut her down. She didn't stop and wag her finger at Jesus, and she didn't allow internalized inferiority complexes to derail her. She listened. She listened as Jesus proclaimed himself the living water. Another thing I like about the woman at the well is that she was an active listener. Active listening involves concentrating on what is being said and making mental or physical notes of the message. Many people are not active listeners. Most of us are preoccupied with crafting our reply during a conversation, which is not really listening.

An active listener is slow to speak and slow to anger. From what we know about this woman, it's possible she didn't understand much of what Jesus was saying, but still, she listened. Active listening also takes patience and effort to understand another person's perspective.

I would say that many people miss out on the blessing that she received from Jesus because they do not listen actively. Jesus told the Samaritan woman, "Everyone who drinks of this water [water from the well] will be thirsty again, but those who drink of the water that I will give them will never be thirsty" (John 4:13–14). He was speaking about the water of eternal life. The woman, who understood the spiritual implications, asked Jesus for his water, for eternal life, so that she may never thirst again. Consider what's going on in this scripture. Consider what this woman was doing. She was listening. If she hadn't been willing to break the cultural taboos and put righteousness first, she never would have been blessed on that day. If she had said, "Well, he's a Judean, and Samaritans and Judeans just don't get along," she would have missed out on a potentially life-changing conversation with the Messiah. Instead, Jesus told her to call her husband and bring him back to the well. We know that the woman said she had no husband, and then Jesus revealed that he knew she had no husband but had had five husbands. She was stunned when Jesus recounted her life story, even pointing out that the man with whom she was currently living was not her husband. At that, she was convinced Jesus was a prophet, and she questioned him about where to worship. She understood that he said that his people must worship in Jerusalem when her ancestors had worshiped on that very mountain (John 4:20).

It should be noted that this was a major contention between the Samaritans and the Judeans: where to worship—on this mount or on that one. She was telling him, *We worship here. You worship in Jerusalem.* She was bringing up a point of contention between their cultures.

> Jesus said to her, "Woman, believe me, the hour is coming when you will worship the Father neither on this mountain

> nor in Jerusalem. You worship what you do not know; we worship what we know, for salvation is from the Jews. But the hour is coming, and is now here, when the true worshipers will worship the Father in spirit and truth, for the Father seeks such as these to worship him. God is spirit, and those who worship him must worship in spirit and truth." The woman said to him, "I know that Messiah is coming" (who is called Christ). "When he comes, he will proclaim all things to us." Jesus said to her, "I am he, the one who is speaking to you."
>
> Just then his disciples came. They were astonished that he was speaking with a woman, but no one said, "What do you want?" or, "Why are you speaking with her?" (John 4:21-27)

The disciples were astonished because Jesus was clearly violating a cultural norm. They weren't surprised. They knew Jesus was committed to putting righteousness first, not tradition or culture. He was going to be righteous even if it made people angry. Jesus did a lot of things he wasn't supposed to do in the culture, particularly concerning the status of women.

Jesus spoke to many women in public. He saved a woman caught in adultery and challenged the powerful men who wanted to judge her. He also counted women like Martha and Mary among his disciples, which, again, was considered by some to be wildly improper in ancient Near Eastern culture. Some rabbis even believed that they weren't supposed to teach women. Jesus not only taught women, but he also had female disciples. What a beautiful scandal that conversation at the well was, because after listening to Jesus's words, she did not hesitate to share what she had heard.

The woman left her jar, the scripture says, not wanting any burden to slow her down as she went back to the city. She announced, "Come and see a man who told me everything I have ever done! He cannot be the Messiah, can he?" (John 4:29–30). She went out and heralded the good news, telling everyone she met about Jesus the Christ. She cried out, "Come and see!" She made the message plain, and people followed her back to Jesus. The text says the people left the city and were on their way to him. In verses 39 to 42, we learn that many Samaritans were blessed because they were willing to listen.

> Many Samaritans from that city believed in him because of the woman's testimony, "He told me everything I have ever done." So when the Samaritans came to him, they asked him to stay with them; and he stayed there two days. And many more believed because of his word. They said to the woman, "It is no longer because of what you said that we believe, for we have heard for ourselves, and we know that this is truly the Savior of the world." (John 4:39–42)

They found Jesus and were blessed with discernment. Imagine if they had been so wrapped up in their culture and traditions that they ignored the woman at the well simply because she was a woman. They would have missed their blessing. I don't know about others, but I'm not about to miss my blessing. If God sends the message through a stranger, like the being Jacob wrestled with, I'm going to listen. If God sends the message through a young child, like David or Joseph, I'm going to listen. If God sends the message through a stone in the desert, like he did with the Hebrew people as they wandered, I'm going to listen.

Many churches struggle today to see the spiritual giftedness with which women are blessed. If God sends the message through a woman, like the woman at the well or like other women mentioned in the Bible—Priscilla, Huldah, Deborah, Philip's daughters, Phoebe, or Eunice—are we going to listen?

Nothing is going to get in the way of us receiving and sharing the message of God if we are willing to listen. Are we listening?

The Power of Listening

In his lectures, former FBI intelligence officer Christopher Voss discusses strategies he used in the field. Regarding negotiation, he says people often talk more than they would like. When we are quiet and listen, he says, the other person in the negotiation will actually reveal themselves. The more you patiently listen, the more they will reveal. When negotiating, he says it's better to be as quiet as possible than to talk too much. This speaks to the power of listening.

As the old saying goes, God gave us two ears and one mouth for a reason.[1] We should listen twice as much as we speak. I think that is a good thing to remember as we go about our daily lives. Most of us would do well to listen more. Listening is often a blessing. Sometimes, folks are trying to tell us things about themselves, but we do not hear them because we do not listen actively, because we don't take into consideration what is being said and what is not being said. Asking clarifying questions is also part of active listening. Consider again the woman at the well questioning Jesus about worship. Her quest for clarification prompted Jesus to reveal more.

Every opportunity to listen is an opportunity to grow. We should listen for nuggets of information that we might need to better ourselves and to better our lives. We will not get that information if we are not listening. Listening is a powerful gift, but it requires a disciplined spirit. To truly listen and hear what another person is saying, we must settle down and let go of the urgency to speak or share an opinion. Imagine the impact on our lives if we apply this technique in our conversations with God.

James tells us: "You must understand this, my beloved: let everyone be quick to listen, slow to speak, slow to anger; for your anger does not produce God's righteousness" (James 1:19–20). This scripture is specifically talking about how we deal with God's Word. It's saying we ought to be quick to listen and slow to anger. The Word of God makes some people angry. We become bitter about God's Word and plan when we try to bring it down to our level rather than lift ourselves toward heaven.

This passage from James 1 can be applied to life in general. Because of our fallen human nature, we carry a lot of baggage with us into conversations. When we try to listen, that baggage influences how we interpret what is being said. Our frames of reference—experiences, upbringing, culture, stereotypes, perception—prevent us from listening objectively to what a person is saying. A person who had harsh and unhelpful teachers might think all teachers are like that. A person who was treated by a condescending and dismissive doctor might think all doctors are the same.

I often run into these stereotypes myself. Many people think they already know me because I am a preacher. They think I'm like the preacher they grew up knowing when they were young. I try to make it clear that we are not all alike and that I am my own person. I have my own walk with God. I am flawed, and I make mistakes.

I travel often and usually by plane. Inevitably, I will strike up a conversation with the person sitting next to me. Typically, we'll start by exchanging names, where we were born and raised, and where we are going. Then comes the question that creates anxiety in me: "What do you do for a living?" I can expect one of two reactions when I say I'm a preacher. I appreciate when the person leans into my expertise and even asks me to help solve some life problems he or she may be experiencing. I am always interested in the types of things people are dealing with, and I'm grateful to be able to help them. Then there's the other typical reaction that I truly abhor: when the person freezes, becomes ice-cold, and looks absolutely terrified. In that person's mind is the recollection of a finger-wagging pastor, or worse. Some people become rigid when meeting a preacher because they assume I'm some type of television charlatan, a prosperity preacher, or someone who seeks to fleece the flock. I constantly deal with this stereotype, especially as an African American male pastor. The entertainment industry often portrays African American clergy, especially male clergy, by this stereotype.

I then have to lean into the conversation to break down walls and persuade people to not fear me. "I wish to walk with you, to be your friend. I have no interest in your money." The rigid responders are often too overwhelmed by the stereotypes embedded in their minds. Most times, I am able to get people to open up and discuss their fears. It's not always easy and requires patience, perseverance, and God's grace.

The board for the Council of Baptist Pastors of Detroit and Vicinity held an event where we used our own resources to bring in scholars to speak to us on relevant topics. Our president at the time was Dr. Steve Bland Jr., and he wanted to advertise the event on social media. He asked me to create a flier and then boost it on Facebook to reach more people. We boosted the flier for two weeks, and it reached more than twenty thousand people. During that time, however, we received many negative comments, such as, "This is what's wrong with the church; they just want more money to buy new fancy suits. They don't care about anyone but themselves." There was no reason for people to say this. The ad was tasteful and professional. No doubt, negative reactions emanated from personal experiences and prejudices. Needless to say, I spent a lot of time on Facebook deleting comments during those two weeks.

We have to listen objectively. If we don't, we might find ourselves going in circles because we will continue to create a world based on our own presuppositions when we should engage with reality instead. Jesus says, "Love your enemies and pray for those who persecute you, so that you may be children of your Father in heaven; for he makes his sun rise on the evil and on the good, and sends rain on the righteous and on the unrighteous" (Matt. 5:44–45).

I lived in Arkansas during Barack Obama's presidency. Arkansas was and still is a solidly red state. I knew folks who said they absolutely would not pray for President Obama because they thought he was the worst. One particular incident that comes to mind involves a distraught classmate. I was studying in the Harding University ministers' lounge when I encountered my frustrated friend. Seeing he had a lot on his mind, I engaged him in conversation. He explained that during Bible study, not one congregant offered prayers for President Obama—something that was done regularly when President George W. Bush was in office—until the night before. Someone actually stood up that night and prayed that President Obama would be assassinated. I tried my best to advise my classmate, although I, too, was in shock. How could anyone, especially someone who professes faith in God, pray to the Prince of Peace for the murder of another human being?

We began to reflect on and pray about the level of political polarization in that region at that time. It often bothers me how some people can be so hateful. I did not understand why the person hated Barack Obama so much. What is doubly baffling is how a person actually thought that God would appreciate their prayers of hatred, because even if the person detested

Barack Obama that much, why not pray for what is best for him, his family, and the country?

In Scripture, Jesus clearly instructs us to pray for the salvation of all souls. We are to pray for everyone, not only those we love and like but also those we detest, those who make us angry, those who annoy us, those who scare us, those who persecute us. We are to pray for our enemies. We are to pray for those people we do not support, do not respect, do not want to be around. It's a tall order, and I don't believe it can be done if we are continually listening from a polarized place; that is, if we allow our preconceptions to shut us down. In fact, we should pray harder for those with whom we disagree. We should pray for God's grace upon all of us, that we might unite in Christ. We have to listen objectively and respond accordingly if we are truly seeking wholeness.

We must also listen humbly. When it comes to listening humbly, consider that most of us have two types of friends. One friend will always tell us what we want to hear but will rarely tell us what we need to hear. We like being around these types of friends because they boost our ego. The other type of friend, a true friend, will sacrifice a relationship with us if telling us what we need to hear benefits us. Because of our fallen nature, we tend to gravitate toward feeding our ego, the friend who tells us what we want to hear.

I believe the world is becoming more and more egocentric because of social media. Social media has inflamed a concept called confirmation bias, the idea that if my ideas—no matter how radical, obscene, or hideous—are confirmed by someone, then I will feel that they are acceptable. Before social media, if we voiced a crazy idea—like the moon is made of cheese—people might laugh and scoff, but it would be hard to find anyone to support that idea. Today, I would almost guarantee that, through the Internet, we could find somebody somewhere who agrees with the idea that the moon is made of cheese.

The world is becoming a place where people cannot handle any type of critique, any type of criticism, any type of idea that may clash with their ideas, any type of different opinions. We're living in a world where people are becoming fragile thanks to concepts like confirmation bias and the popularity of social media. When people disagree, they shun each other instead of pursuing truth together. They shun each other and seek out silos of people who will confirm their beliefs.

I've started trying my best to learn how to be a radical listener. I am a type A personality. I tend to speak very directly and say exactly what I mean. However, I've come to understand that not everyone communicates this way. Some people speak indirectly, assuming others will pick up their subtleties and derive meaning from what is not being said. I believe this is a cultural or perhaps geographical difference. Whatever the reason or origin, I learned by moving to different regions of the United States that I had to communicate in others' styles instead of my own. I had to learn to listen with all my senses, not just my ears, and I needed to ask questions for clarification. I also learned that my direct approach might be off-putting to others. The bottom line is that I came to the realization that, to be an effective communicator, I have to adapt my communication style to my audience's style—whether it's an audience of one or many. This takes practice, and I have some ways to go, but it is just another way to be a radical listener.

I continually work to harness and engage the power of listening. Being a radical listener requires listening first to understand as opposed to listening to respond. Radical listening means that I listen with self-awareness. I listen with awareness of my own biases, triggers, and passions, and I do my best to not allow any of the three to corrupt the message I receive. Also, when we listen radically, we listen to determine truth, not to win a debate. For instance, if someone offers advice or an opinion that we might not necessarily agree with, we should ask for further clarification or an example. Ask, "Can you help me to understand what you mean?" Perhaps draw more out of the other person by saying, "I want to explore that with you," or simply ask, "Why?"

The end goal is not to build up ego and feel like the best thing since sliced bread. I like to learn more so that I become the best version of myself. I want to be as obedient to God as much as possible, so whenever I receive the gift of information, even in the form of critique or criticism, I consider how it is going to help me become a better person. I accept it with a glad heart, and I may ask for help in investigating it even further.

James tells us, "You must understand this, my beloved: let everyone be quick to listen, slow to speak, slow to anger; for your anger does not produce God's righteousness. Therefore rid yourselves of all sordidness and rank growth of wickedness, and welcome with meekness the implanted word" (James 1:19–21).

We cannot get the implanted Word if we are prideful and arrogant. If we know any truth, it's only because God has revealed it to us. God is the absolute source of all absolute truth.

What must we do to listen to what God is trying to tell us? Hebrews says, "Do not forget to entertain strangers, for by so doing some have unwittingly entertained angels" (Heb. 13:2 NKJV). *Angel* comes from the Greek word *angelos*, which means "messenger." We might have entertained one of God's messengers who was trying to bring an absolute truth from God, but because we were too prideful and arrogant, we were not able to receive it.

Christians must also listen intently. Proverbs 18:13 says, "If one gives answer before hearing, it is folly and shame." A lot of people, when it's time to listen, are so eager to respond they don't even hear what the messenger is saying. According to Proverbs, that is folly and shame.

Listen first not to simply let the other person get his or her thought out until it is your turn to speak but to understand the message by processing the words in the right context. Then, clarify the message to show respect before sharing a response.

Businessman, author, and motivational speaker Stephen R. Covey writes, "Most people do not listen with the intent to understand; they listen with the intent to reply."[2] Poet Maya Angelou once said, "When someone shows you who they are, believe them the first time." Sometimes, we cannot hear what a person is saying about who they are because we aren't really listening. Think about two people arguing from the exact same position. It's likely each of us has been in this type of discussion at some point. The issue at hand is not the crux of the confrontation. The fact that neither party is listening to the other is at the root of the problem. So many arguments could be avoided if we seek first to listen, then to understand, and then to find and focus on areas of agreement.

Finally, we must listen to God. We must listen divinely. The Bible tells us, "But he said, 'Blessed rather are those who hear the word of God and obey it!'" (Luke 11:28). Affirming the lesson in James 1, those who hear the Word of God and obey it are blessed. James describes how necessary it is for those who learn from the Word to not merely hear it but to act upon it. As we listen divinely to what God is saying to us and act upon it, we will not forget the Word of the Lord and how to obey God (James 1:22–25).

I wonder how there can be so many people in the world who call themselves believers in God, yet the world has not transformed from the way of evil to the way of goodness. The answer I always seem to land on is that too many people call themselves believers but are not doers. We must be hearers and doers. If we truly believe, then doing should come naturally. Right?

Conversely, problems arise when we are hyper-focused on doing, because we may fail to slow down and listen. Studying the Word of God requires laying down our baggage so those burdens do not affect our understanding of what God is trying to tell us.

True study of God's Word will move us, challenge us, make us cry, frustrate us, and cause us to wonder. It will also remind us to say to ourselves, "I can do it by the grace of God and by the power of the Holy Spirit." I strongly encourage anyone who has never had that experience before to start listening to the Word. As the Bible tells us in Romans 10:17 (KJV), "So then faith cometh by hearing, and hearing by the Word of God."

There's a great deal of power in listening—gospel power. The power of God is in listening.

Reflection Questions

▶ What habits can we form to become better listeners?

▶ How can listening be virtuous?

▶ What virtues can we pray for when praying to be a better listener?

▶ Describe a time when you were appreciated for listening actively. How did that make you feel?

▶ What are some things we can do to let a speaker know we are listening rather than just hearing?

Notes

[1] This saying is thought to have originated with the Greek stoic philosopher Epictetus.

[2] Stephen R. Covey, *The 7 Habits of Highly Effective People: Powerful Lessons in Personal Change* (New York: Simon and Schuster, 1989), 239.

2

THE SPIRITUAL RECIPE
Prayer, Fasting, and Study

One of the joys of waking up in the morning is having a new day ahead. No matter how bad yesterday was, we have a chance to make the new day better. In every way and by every definition, the day ahead is a God-given opportunity. It's an opportunity to work, laugh, heal, learn, and improve. A new day is an opportunity for growth.

Let's consider this idea of growth. There are, after all, many types of growth. Some growths, such as cancer, are unhealthy. The physical growth and maturation we witness in children, however, is natural and healthy. As Christians, who are called to share the Lord's Word, we are in the business of growing our relationships, our missions, and our congregations. Spiritual growth and renewal can be transformative and life-changing. Spiritual growth is never-ending. We should continually strive to grow spiritually.

Among the congregants at my previous church was a young man who did not take his faith or relationship with God seriously. The problem was not only that he did not appreciate the sacred, but also that he did not take anything in life seriously. It is no coincidence that a believer who does not place much stock in faith will also wander about life with a cavalier attitude. Despite my best efforts to impress upon him the gravity of his faith walk, his education, his familial relationships, and his professional calling, it took a life-changing event to wake him up.

I received a horrific phone call one day. This young man had been in a serious accident on a busy highway. I dropped what I was doing and went straight to the hospital. He was in bad shape, fighting for his life. His car had flipped several times. His mother was sick with worry, and I tried to comfort her, explaining that her son had much to live for. I spoke to him as well, even though he was unconscious. I assured him of my prayers that when he regained consciousness, he would live with renewed purpose. By the grace of God, he was discharged from the hospital after several months. His recovery was a long, arduous road, but he faced it with hope and perseverance. He turned his life around following that accident.

I recall the first time he was physically able to attend services again. He walked into church that Sunday, and the congregation clapped and cheered for him. A new man, he began to take all of his relationships seriously. He went back to school and learned a trade. He showed appreciable respect for his family and his faith, and he attended church regularly on Sundays. It took looking death in the eye for this man to realize how precious life is. He was fortunate to survive the crash and have the opportunity to fulfill his faith calling, putting to good use the gifts God had given him. He began sharing his faith with others. As it turned out, he had an extensive network. Having been an athlete, he had the ear of his teammates, so he was able to influence people of all ages. Witnessing his transformation encouraged me to share all the more the importance of growing in faith, because no matter where we are on our faith journey, there is always room for growth. We cannot rest on our laurels, for "the Lord will come like a thief in the night" (1 Thess. 5:2).

I was grateful to God that this young man turned his life around and was now an active foot soldier for the Lord. He made a positive impression on many, including me, but I never fully realized the impact my ministry had on him until he thanked me for helping him grow in faith and take it more seriously. He later provided a testimonial for my ministry. This is yet another example of why we should be ever mindful of how we live our lives; whether we realize it or not, our actions and words influence those around us. It is important to encourage one another.

The apostle Paul assured the Christians in Corinth that their struggles would make them stronger and better. "So we do not lose heart. Even though our outer nature is wasting away, our inner nature is being renewed day by day" (2 Cor. 4:16). Paul was well aware of how easy it was to become discouraged when facing physical and emotional trials, but he told the Christians in Corinth that, during those struggles, they were being replenished and improved. Pause and think about this. Is it possible to grow without a little struggle? Any kind of growth requires change, and that change can sometimes be difficult.

Take, for instance, working out and getting into shape. If we want to grow and improve our physical fitness, we're going to struggle. We're going to sweat and feel some pain. If we want to grow in learning or further our education, we're going to tax our brains and stay up late at night studying. If we want to grow in wisdom, I think there are two ways to proceed. One way is by listening to the wise, and the other is by attending the school of hard knocks. Whatever path we choose, growing in wisdom requires sacrifice.

The thing about life in general is that everyone, Christians and non-Christians alike, must grow. We should all end in a different place from where we started. As Christians, we have a special mandate for growth because we want to grow closer and closer to God and to Jesus Christ. Even Jesus grew through the years, increasing in wisdom and in divine and human favor (Luke 2:52). I realized that if Jesus could grow, there's no excuse for me not to grow. There's no excuse for any of us not to grow if Jesus himself had to grow.

I believe God has called each of us to grow in mind, grow in love for the church, and grow in spirit. We should, therefore, try to supplement our faith with virtue, knowledge, self-control, steadfastness, godliness, brotherly affection, and love (2 Pet. 1:5–7). I love this passage from 2 Peter 1 because it exemplifies growth. Peter is showing us here that we should not simply claim our Christian faith and then stand still. We must continually move forward. We must add to that faith, virtue, or goodness. To that virtue, we must add knowledge, and then we must temper that knowledge with self-control. To our self-control we must bring steadfastness, or commitment. With that commitment, we must exhibit godliness, and in godliness, we must embrace brotherly affection until we arrive at a deep and abiding love. Arriving at a deep and abiding love is akin to arriving at a destination when traveling. The process is the -ing. That's the continuous action that leads us to our destination.

When a romantic couple says "I love you" for the first time, they are not fully demonstrating the depth of love they can establish for one another. As years go by and they weather triumphs and tragedies together—having children, burying older relatives, marking milestones—"I love you" takes on a deeper meaning. It encompasses all their shared experiences, and it acknowledges each other's shortcomings, blessings, and everything in between. To a seasoned couple, "I love you" expresses affirmation of the commitment the two made during their early, hopeful years of courtship. That's what Paul was referring to when he wrote about the process of getting to this deep love and affection.

As we grow in heart, we grow in mind, which God clearly wants us to do. While Paul said that knowledge can be problematic and can create inflated egos, he said that, when coupled with virtue and self-control, pursuit of knowledge is humbling.

In some Christian circles, people have intentionally and openly opposed the pursuit of knowledge. There has been anti-intellectualism, with some leaders discouraging freethinking. When I was growing up, the number one sentence in my home was "Why?" My parents encouraged my sister and me to be inquisitive, and they did all they could to provide answers to our questions. That included the nice *Encyclopedia Britannica* set they bought from the door-to-door salesman. They also took us to the library frequently. I can hear my mother clearly to this day responding to my questions: "Look it up." That classic response was frustrating, but it taught me how to research.

I recall sitting in my room one day thinking and then instantly being overcome by a chilling feeling. I was only nine years old at the time. The question that caused the hair on the back of my neck to stand up was, "Where did God come from?" When I was a young boy, my thought process was one of causal relationships. *If I had a mommy and daddy, did God? And if God had a mom and dad, who were their moms and dads?* As I ruminated, I became quite concerned, and then I asked my parents. While the questions gave me chills, they made my parents proud. I remember thinking their reaction was strange. I later realized they were proud because I was thinking like a theologian. Coincidentally, or not, I became a theologian.

My parents took me to our church to speak with our minister about my concern. I recall the minister using an illustration that I thought was over-the-top. It involved a soda can, which I didn't quite understand, but I managed to take from his demonstration the fact that God is eternal and that while God has given us divine attributes, God is not us. My biological existence requires a mother and father, but God's eternal existence does not. This revelation was not clear to me at the moment because I was confused by the soda can (and still am). When we left the meeting, my parents asked if I felt better. I told them I did but that I still had a lot of thinking to do. Over the following weeks, using some of the tools I got from that meeting, I was able to process and understand God's eternal nature. This is the blessing of being a free and critical thinker and honestly asking and exploring questions.

I have no doubt that the reality of God is valid. This is a truth claim, and truth can withstand scrutiny. Truth only becomes stronger every time it conquers scrutiny.

Growing in knowledge is clearly part of our Christian walk. We have a responsibility to pursue the knowledge of God, a knowledge of divine things, a knowledge of all things holy, and a knowledge of things pure.

The Bible says to love God with "all your heart." Check. Love God with "all your soul." Check. Love God with all your body. Check. The Bible also says to love God "with all your mind" (Mark 12:30). That means that to be Christians, we cannot check our minds at the door. God gave us that mind, and God wants us to use it to grow in knowledge.

God is all-powerful, and his love for us is one of God's all-powerful attributes. This is unlike Satan, who doesn't have any power, with the exception of the power of his lies. Too many people assume that the devil has a lot of power, but he does not! The devil is not omnipotent or omniscient. The devil does not have all knowledge. He is not all-powerful. Sometimes, when we talk about the devil, we talk like the devil is all-knowing, but the devil is not. The devil has some information but not all of it. Only God, Yahweh, is the alpha and the omega and knows all things. Sometimes when we talk about the evil one, we talk about him as if he is all-powerful, but he's not. Compared to our God, the devil is a weakling.

Yet, he does exert a certain power. The devil's power is found in his lies. He is cunning. The devil is the king of lies. The devil tricks folks into believing in lies. In fact, the word *devil* in Greek means the deceiver, the one who deceives you. How can we avoid falling into the trap of a lie? By growing in knowledge. It's hard to trap somebody who isn't afraid to grow in knowledge, but the devil is able to win when there's apathy and no love for the oracles of God. When Christians are not growing in knowledge, any lie can supplant truth. We must grow in knowledge and in understanding—not only because it's what God wants us to do, but also because it's how we protect ourselves from the lies of the evil one.

God's will for us is to grow in love for the church by being kind and forgiving one another just as God has forgiven us (Eph. 4:32). I'm not talking about being fixated with our bricks and mortar, although it's fine to appreciate them. I'm talking about growing in love for our brothers and sisters, the people who sit in the pews beside us. We must grow because relationships that do not grow and adjust and mature will wither. Growing in love for God's church is the very way we grow God's church. By his own design, love is a powerful tool of outreach. John 13:35 says the world shall know that we are Christ's disciples by how we love each other.

Think about John 3:16: "For God so loved the world that he gave his only Son." To love each other, to grow in love, is to grow closer to the heart of God, who is love.

God also wishes for his people, his church, to grow in spirit, so that we may unite in eternity. As humans created by God, we exist and live in fleshly bodies, but we were created in God's image, which means there's a trace of God within each of us. This acts as a homing device calling us toward God. We were created as spiritual beings to pursue fruits of the Holy Spirit. God gave us free will, however, so that our desire and pursuit of him would be pure. This creates in each of us a constant struggle between the flesh and the spirit.

We often want and are sorely tempted to live like other mammals, putting the flesh first. We might be tempted to use our might or our prowess or our carnal strength to get what we want. We might be tempted to go tit for tat with people or an eye for an eye with others, but God's plan for us is to live by the Holy Spirit.

How do we grow in spirituality? In 1 Thessalonians 5:17, we are instructed to pray without ceasing, saying we should talk to God all the time. Mother Teresa, famous for ministering to the poor of Calcutta, India, also ministered to others. As the story goes, a businessman sought her counsel regarding his fledgling enterprise and his limited capacity to meet his various obligations, including his payroll. He was suffering from severe stress. Mother Teresa advised him to simply spend more time in prayer. She did not tell him to pray for more time or more revenue or to work longer hours. Just the opposite, she advised him to spend more time with God.

Think about all the time we spend on our cell phones. In 2018, *Inc.* magazine reported that the average person logged more than four hours of screen time per day.[1] Most smartphones offer the option in the settings application to track our screen time. I suspect the number of hours might come as a shock to many of us. What if we spent some or even all that time in prayer? What might change in our lives or in the lives of those around us? How much closer might we grow to God and his will for us? It's certainly a nice thought, but it's far more than that. It requires work. Praying is a spiritual discipline. That means we must practice it intentionally and consistently with focus and commitment.

At the same time, it's important for us to realize that we aren't alone in our pursuit of spiritual disciplines. God has provided us with a helper, a spiritual guide. Matthew 4:1 says, "Then Jesus was led up by the Spirit." If we're being led by the Holy Spirit, the Holy Spirit is going to lead us to do some healthy things. The Holy Spirit will not lead us to do things that are going to harm us or be toxic to our spirit. The Holy Spirit leads us to do things that are going to nourish our souls. Jesus was led by the Holy Spirit into the desert, where he fasted for forty days and forty nights. We know that while he was there, he was tempted by Satan. Satan knew that Jesus was in the desert to fulfill God's will and grow even closer to God, and he did not like it. Satan does not like it when we try to grow in our spirituality. Know that when we try to pray without ceasing, Satan is going to be in our minds, trying to influence us. Make no mistake, Satan will sow the seeds of doubt, and we might find ourselves saying, "Well, how can I do it? How can I pray without ceasing? I have stuff to do in life. It's not possible." We might start to procrastinate, pushing our prayer time to the next day and then the day after that until the week is gone and we're back to Sunday. We sometimes view our spirituality like our finances—paycheck to paycheck. Sunday to Sunday is when we pray. Sunday to Sunday is when we read the Scriptures. Sunday to Sunday is when we spend time with the saints. Doesn't God call us to more than that?

Paul tells us to present our bodies as living sacrifices (Rom. 12:1). Everything we have should be dedicated to God. Financial management is very important, but as important as it is, time management is more important, because if we do not manage time, we will not be able to manage the rest of our lives, including our spiritual lives. Within time management, it is critical that we make time for our spiritual life. In fact, it is critical that we put prayer first and trust that God will guide us as we manage the rest of our time.

Jesus lived this way. Remember that he walked into the desert to fast. Fasting is a spiritual discipline, and it does not always have to involve abstaining from food. We can abstain from screen time. We can abstain from television. We can abstain from something that may have a hold on us so that we can regain control. We can abstain from something that might be a growing idol in our hearts. Fast from it. Turn away from it.

Another spiritual discipline that helps us grow closer to God is giving to others. If we give generously to one another, we will not lose our eternal reward (Matt. 10:42). We find here that even the act of giving to others brings us closer to Christ. We live in a world where greed is often considered virtuous.

I witnessed this during one of my first jobs as a teenager. Being young, I was willing to take any job I could get. I landed at one of those rent-to-own centers. I learned a lot about society there. On the surface, this seemed like a valiant business because it enabled people to rent appliances they could not afford to purchase outright. Customers could pay weekly or monthly installments on things like washing machines, refrigerators, televisions, and furniture. It did not take me long to realize that this business model only benefited the lender. The borrowers ended up paying as much as five times the value of any particular product. They were being robbed and did not even realize it. Making matters worse, our typical customers were poor people who lived in humble environments and could least afford to waste money. Not all were of that ilk, but most lacked the financial literacy to understand how they were being exploited. I recall processing the callousness of an organization willing to take advantage of individuals. Adding insult to injury, customers would often request payment arrangements, which is standard practice for any borrower, even the wealthy. At this establishment, however, the manager was more than happy to make arrangements, knowing well that he was signing people up for a lifelong debt cycle that would enrich him. "Sure, we can work with you," he'd say, with a sinister smile. "Just sign here."

Before long, I was disgusted by the practice and chose to leave the company and take a job at a local bookstore. I took a pay cut, too. Not only was I earning less, but I also ended up spending much of my earnings on books, even though I enjoyed a generous employee discount. I devoured countless books, and I began buying books to give as gifts. Despite my meager earnings and the money I spent on books, that job was a blessing because it was an investment in my education—academic and worldly. I learned at a young age that there are pros and cons to everything. In a capitalistic society, where generating capital is necessary, we must be careful to not pursue capital for the love of capital, or the love of money, but for the greater good. Love of money can lead us to a corrupted vision of humanity, of ourselves, and ultimately of how we are to interact with one another. We must take care of each other and "seek first the kingdom of God" (Matt. 6:33 CSB). Such spiritual discipline brings God's grace upon us, freeing us from the sin of selfishness. God calls us to be compassionate and to give of our time, talent, and treasure. Like any discipline, this requires practice, work.

This Christian work, this growth, is important, but while engaging in it, we must remember all the ministries we are called to, such as the ministries of stewardship over our bodies (health), spending time and taking care of our families, and enriching our own personal devotional life with God.

I went to Ghana in 2017 because I had traveled to the south of Africa and the east of Africa but never the west. I wanted to see the west of Africa because that was the closest direct connection to my heritage. I also have ancestors from South and East Africa, but those roots are more ancient. As I mentioned previously, my classmates Vincent and Benjamin and I raised money to fund this venture. My prior trips were paid for by my university.

In Ghana, I taught for a month. Of all the subjects I taught, the concept of putting oneself before one's work was the most controversial because Africans have a tremendous work ethic. The idea of self-care was new and radical to them. They had no interest in putting their own well-being before their tasks. The Ghanaians with whom I worked were very close to the earth—literally. They worked the land. Such a concept is probably foreign to many Americans, many of whom, I suspect, live in an illusion by thinking food comes from a grocery store. My students brought to the forefront of my mind something I had observed throughout life: the closer we are to the earth, the stronger our work ethic is.

I could relate to the Ghanaians because I also struggled with the idea of taking care of myself; I thought that I was doing a good thing by putting all my energy into ministry, even if my own spirit was malnourished. I thought it was good to work myself to the bone, even if my spirit was starving. When I took a closer look at Luke 5:15–16, I began to change my thinking: "Yet the news about him spread all the more, so that crowds of people came to hear him and to be healed of their sicknesses. But Jesus often withdrew to lonely places and prayed" (NIV). I read this and said, "Wow!" This is telling us that even during our busiest seasons, we have to take a break to pray for our own spiritual nourishment.

I share this point for readers who are working for the Lord. The faithful servant of God might sometimes feel overstretched. Perhaps they are exhausted, and their own prayer life might be suffering. I want everyone to know that is not what God wants for us, regardless of our vocation. God wants us to serve, yes. God wants us to minister, yes. God does not want us to neglect our own prayer life, though. We must do as Jesus did. Wake up early in the morning before the crowd and take time for ourselves, away from others. Seek out the quiet and solitude. Seek God's voice and spend time in prayer. Spend time to make sure our souls are all right with God. Such time will never be a waste.

Growth is not always easy. It brings with it pain and anxiety but also great joy and wonder. Growth is ever-present because we, as Christians, are flawed people. We will always have room to grow, not only as individuals, but also as a collective group. The beautiful part about growing in spirituality is that God has already provided us with all the resources we need to get started. Through the Holy Spirit, each of us is capable of growing in mind, in our love for the church, and in spirit. Do not be afraid. Let's embrace growth.

Humility

In the book *The Vulnerable Pastor*, author Mandy Smith tells a story of a mountaineer named Joe Simpson. She shares this from Simpson's memoir, *Touching the Void*:

> Thousands of feet up the side of the Siula Grande mountain, Joe's safety line was cut, leaving Joe to slide with a broken leg into a deep crevasse. After several desperate attempts to climb up and out of the crevasse, he was faced with the fact that his injury made it impossible. And so, against all survival instinct, he made the excruciating choice to lower himself deeper into the crevasse in the hope that there would be other exits farther down, all the time wondering, "Am I lowering myself to freedom or deeper into the belly of the earth? Does a ray of sunlight await me in the pit, showing a way out into day, or is there only darkness and slow death?" With every inch he lowered himself down, he edged farther from the obvious way to life—and there was no way back up.[2]

Obviously, Simpson made the right decision, because he lived to share his harrowing experience. The story illustrates a sort of surrender we must embrace if we are to have any sort of breakthrough regarding our work for the kingdom of God. Smith writes, "What if, instead of this futile effort to inch into the pretense of fullness, we made a counterintuitive, countercultural choice? What if we chose to lower ourselves, to defy every survival instinct and start emptying?"

Many of us tend to be centrally focused, putting our own interests above all else. Smith challenges us to go against that tendency, to swim against the cultural tide. Our culture advocates selfishness. It encourages us to do what makes us feel good, whatever brings us the most success, the most wealth regardless of how it affects others. Nature tells us something similar. When a lion sees a zebra, it doesn't care if that zebra has babies. The lion acts on instinct—seeing easy prey, it launches its attack. The lion does not ask ethical questions. All it knows is that it is hungry and the zebra or her babies are food. Of course, there's a huge difference between the animal kingdom and humankind.

In Genesis, God had before him the entire animal kingdom. He chose to set apart the human species, as we were made in God's likeness. While we have that divinity, we also have features similar to animals, such as the digestive system, reproductive system, nervous system, and the like. We have a conscience and the ability to reason. We also have free choice, by the grace of God. It is up to us to decide whether we want to project the image of God or the image of animals.

To be countercultural, or counterintuitive to our survival instincts, is to automatically reject the animal image. Choose the image of God instead of the animal. Being countercultural is choosing God over the crowd. The path will not always be easy, but it will certainly lead to eternal rewards.

Pray about it. Ask him to teach us his paths and to lead us in truth, for he is our salvation. Ask him to remember the mercy he has for us and not remember the sins of our youth but rather his steadfast love for us (Ps. 25:4–7).

Consider the life of David. Many scholars believe David wrote Psalm 25 during his own time of chaos, the time of his son Absalom's rebellion. This was a trying time for David, who was unaware that he was lost. His son was actively working to overthrow his kingdom and wanted to see him finished. The reason Absalom was so upset was because David had done wrong. Tamar, Absalom's sister, David's daughter, was violated in the most intimate way by her half-brother Amnon, and David did not seek justice for his daughter, Tamar. Absalom became angry and vowed to take it upon himself to exact justice. Absalom was seeking to avenge Tamar by going after Amnon as well as David.

It is clear that David was confused. He was lost. He was making all sorts of mistakes, and he finally settled down and went to the Lord for help and direction. "Make me to know your ways, O Lord; teach me your paths" (Ps. 25:4 ESV). David's words came from a place of deep sorrow for having been betrayed and for committing the act of betrayal. He was lost and casting about for answers, for guidance.

What is interesting about being lost is that not everybody who wanders knows they are lost. Think about it. When do we become lost? Many of us walk our paths utterly lost, of course, but are convinced we are headed in the right direction. How do we know when we are lost? Sometimes, it takes trauma to shake us out of our stupor. Sometimes it takes suffering. It starts with that awful feeling in our stomachs. Maybe it is just one butterfly, but before we know it, it feels like a hundred butterflies, and we realize, "Something is not right. I don't recognize where I am. I don't recognize what I'm doing." Maybe we do not even recognize ourselves, and then just like that, we say, "I am lost!"

There are not too many things that are as frustrating as getting lost. It doesn't matter if we're on foot, on a bike, or in a car. Getting lost can be frustrating, tiring, time-consuming, and at times even dangerous. It does not take very long to appreciate direction. It does not take very long before we long and wish for direction. Before the advent of GPS systems, we typically sought and found someone to ask when we needed directions.

Some people are too prideful to ask for help, though. Some prefer guarding their pride and remaining lost over having the humility to find direction. Unfortunately, this is similar to how we often approach God. When God sends us direction or sends someone into our lives to help us find direction, we are usually already lost. It is a joy and comfort to know where we are going, especially if we have been lost for a long time.

In Homer's *Odyssey*, Odysseus traveled the mythical world. He became lost on his journey and encountered all kinds of dangers, including sirens, the Cyclopes, and sea monsters. Not to mention the occasions when he angered the false mythical rulers of the elements of nature, provoking them to become angry with him and make his plight even tougher. When Odysseus finally got directions home, he was so happy that his troubles were all behind him. It was like his troubles were far in his past because he had finally found direction for how to get home. Now, the story of the *Odyssey* is fallacious. Odysseus made an appeal to false gods for help finding direction in a fictional story, but we, the children of God, are blessed because we serve the real God. Not Zeus. Not Horus. We serve the God of Abraham, and we are blessed because we serve the real God who offers real direction. He allows us to follow. We serve a God of salvation. It is a blessing to receive God's directions.

After we realize we are lost, as David did, we must make a choice. We can continue to follow our current path and keep wandering aimlessly, or we can ask God for direction. That is the point David had reached in Psalm 25. He was beseeching God, asking him to reveal his ways, his paths. Sometimes, a request like that requires so much humility that we would rather wander aimlessly than say, "God, show me the way." We can be like the stereotypical movie husband who insists he knows where he's going while his equally stereotypical wife badgers him to stop and ask for directions. We don't want to ask God for directions because to ask God for directions is submission. It's an admission of helplessness. It's saying, "I need help. My way isn't working."

Today, there is a war on truth. There is a war on God's wisdom. David, despite having done awful things, still had the good sense to ask God to lead him in truth and teach him. This is a beautiful prayer: "Make me to know your ways, O LORD; teach me your paths. Lead me in your truth, and teach me, for you are the God of my salvation" (Ps. 25:4–5). I'm going to issue a warning here: be careful when praying this prayer. When praying this prayer, be prepared for God's ways and have faith. Be not afraid, but be prepared.

There is a godly wisdom, and God teaches us through it. That means all the mercy God has shown us thus far is the same mercy that God has shown his people for ages. Even when we make terrible, sinful choices, as David did, God is not done with us. We must be participants in that redemption, however, and we must be willing to wait on the Lord, even if it takes all day or all year.

We sometimes get into trouble because we just don't want to wait. We give it a good five minutes and then throw up our hands, saying, "Okay, now I'm doing it my way." When that happens, our aimless wandering continues, our mistakes pile up, and we have the propensity to do more damage to ourselves and to those around us. If we wait on God—and no, it is not easy—God will reveal his paths.

One way to get better at waiting on God is to accept God's leadership in our lives. We must remember God's innate goodness and faithfulness and humbly accept God's truth and wisdom.

Growing up, I had a dog named Sergeant. Sergeant was a very hardheaded dog. He was hard to train, he was disobedient, and my parents didn't like him. Sergeant's life could have been much better if he had been a little bit more obedient. Later, we got another dog, which my mother decided to name Lady McDainty. A very strange name and so embarrassing. People would ask, "What's your dog's name?" And I would mutter, completely mortified, "The dog's name is Lady McDainty."

The thing about Lady McDainty is that she was extremely obedient. She followed instructions, learned tricks, and was easily house-trained. As a result, my parents got Lady McDainty everything she wanted. And I mean everything. The dog had everything because she was so obedient. She reaped the blessings of humility. Imagine how easy it is for God to bless us when we come to God humbly. It's not that God doesn't wish to bless the prideful; it's that it's harder to bless the prideful because the prideful sometimes think they don't need anything. The prideful sometimes don't even believe they need God. In so many ways, it's the prideful who get in the way of their own blessings. Lady McDainty was conditioned to be obedient. God loves us so much that he gave us the blessing of free will, which alone should cause us to want to choose obedience to God.

David's prayer in Psalm 25 also demonstrates another step that we, as followers of God, must take to truly learn God's ways. In verse 7, he wrote, "Remember not the sins of my youth or my transgressions; according to your steadfast love remember me, for the sake of your goodness, O LORD!" (ESV). David passionately asked God to overlook the sins of his youth—the failures, the errors, the lapses of judgment, the thoughtless transgressions. He asked for forgiveness. Such forgiveness will make clear to all the essential goodness of God.

Many of us have things in our youth we are not proud of. Some of us are ashamed about things we did in our youth. We must remember we serve a God who is eager for us to repent. We serve a God who is willing to save us from ourselves and show us mercy and steadfast love and kindness, but we must be willing to repent.

Imagine having a prideful friend and a humble friend. The prideful friend is always talking about how great she is and all the stuff she knows and has and does. The humble friend listens more than he speaks, is slow to anger, and rarely calls attention to himself. To which friend would we be more eager to give advice? The humble friend, of course.

We also must ask ourselves in what direction our compass is set. Chew on this question: *In what direction is my compass set?* If we have a compass, we can never really get lost. The key to having direction is having a reliable compass and using it.

When we're walking toward God, we might be tempted to turn around and head in an old direction because that's how we've always done things. That's what we know. It's comfortable. We must get out of our comfort zones. We will be tempted to stray off course, but we must keep walking toward God.

We must ask ourselves: *Where is my compass set? Is my compass set to pragmatism or functionalism? Is my compass set to my fleshly desires? Is my compass set to the easy way, or is my compass set to God's way?* I say we should keep pushing toward God and let no sirens, no sea monsters, no lust, no storms, nothing keep us from God's way. Nothing. Keep moving forward. Let's set our compasses toward God. If we do, even when we veer off, it's so much easier to pray this prayer that David prayed to ask for help:

> Make me to know your ways, O Lord; teach me your paths. Lead me in your truth and teach me, for you are the God of my salvation; for you I wait all the day long. Remember your mercy, O Lord, and your steadfast love, for they have been from of old. Remember not the sins of my youth or my transgressions; according to your steadfast love remember me. (Ps. 25:4–7 ESV)

Every new day is a chance to start over, set our compass, and walk with God. Whatever happens, whether the day brings joys, sorrows, temptations, or victories, we are called to keep on walking.

⟹ Reflection Questions ⟸

▶ Why is the concept of change scary, and what are some things we can do to overcome that fear?

▶ Describe a situation where change for the sake of change can only be debilitating and stunt a person's growth.

▶ What can we do to keep our egos in check?

▶ Make a list of all the ways we can work prayer into every aspect of our daily lives.

- Think of a time when you were lost. Was your first reaction to ask for directions, or were you determined to figure out the puzzle on your own?

- Think of a time when you were betrayed, or think of someone you know who has been betrayed. Was your immediate reaction to pray, or did bitterness take over? How can we mentally prepare to react to such indignations with a prayerful heart?

Notes

[1] Melanie Curtin, "Are You On Your Phone Too Much?: The Average Person Spends This Many Hours On It Every Day," *Inc.*, October 30, 2018, https://www.inc.com/melanie-curtin/are-you-on-your-phone-too-much-average-person-spends-this-many-hours-on-it-every-day.html/.

[2] Mandy Smith, *The Vulnerable Pastor: How Human Limitations Empower Our Ministry* (Downers Grove, IL: InterVarsity Press, 2015), 52.

3

ACCEPTING CONTENTMENT

"I can do all things through Christ who strengthens me" (Phil. 4:13 NKJV) is one of the most quoted verses in the Bible. It is often heard at sporting events where athletes are predicting their success on the field. Some people even cite it when they are up for a promotion or before they sit for an exam, predicting their professional and academic successes. While it's wonderful to feel inspired by this scripture, we can misunderstand the true context. I believe the apostle Paul stated a truth that can bring us a great deal of hope in uncertain times—times like we are currently living in. There is a lot to navigate in today's world: civil unrest, racial injustice, indiscriminate gun violence, financial inequality, a post-pandemic society. Many people are wondering, "Is God still good?" They are struggling with their faith and asking hard questions of God—and of those who claim to be God's people.

To fully understand Paul's meaning, we must delve into Philippians 4:10–14. In this passage, he was addressing the church at Philippi and a gift the people had given to him. He wrote his praises to the Lord for the generosity that these people had shown him and how greatly the Lord had provided through this struggle. Paul wrote how he had come to be happier with whatever he had, as he knew what it was like to have little and plenty. He proved in this passage that by relying on God, enduring various circumstances becomes possible. Paul was speaking about finding contentment in any of life's circumstances. It might not seem fair to ask people to be content in crisis situations, but remember that being content does not mean becoming dishonest or complacent, but trusting in God.

What I mean is that if we are in pain, it's okay to say so. If we are lonely, it's okay to express it. If we are suffering, it's okay to admit it. Contentment is about finding calm and peace and a certain degree of acceptance within a circumstance. It is about leveling ourselves so we can remain guided by the Holy Spirit instead of acting out of fear and desperation. When we find contentment, we are able to remember that Jesus Christ is present even amid crises.

Today, many of us are riddled with fear. In the United States alone, our strong economy has faced struggles, our healthcare system seems overburdened, conspiracy theories are rampant, and science is under attack from multiple fronts. There are devils right in front of us, but we ignore them because we are too busy chasing the esoteric. For example, in 2020, a friend insisted that the novel coronavirus was planted in China by then President Trump so he would have a reason to cancel the presidential elections and remain in office indefinitely. I told my friend that I did not think this was the case and that I planned on remaining calm, trusting in God, and focusing on God's will. My friend seemed bothered that I was not nearly as alarmed about the possibility that this theory was accurate.

The very next day, I received a call from another friend who told me the virus was a hoax perpetrated by the Democrats to stop President Trump from winning reelection. I told this friend that I did not think this was so and that I was not alarmed but was placing my trust in God.

To all who are full of fear, I say, *Let God's will be done.* We can and should solve the problems God wants us to solve, but there is little point in worrying over something God hasn't called us to worry about. We are of much better use serving people in need, advocating for the voiceless, and helping our communities unite for the common good. We are of much better use taking care of the business God has set before us. In doing this, we can move ever closer to contentment. When we are content, we trust God and do not get dragged down into the mental and spiritual chaos of fear and loathing.

The fear and uncertainty I am seeing in so many circles reminds me of what Jesus said in Matthew 24:3–8:

> When he was sitting on the Mount of Olives, the disciples came to him privately, saying, "Tell us, when will this be, and what will be the sign of your coming and of the end of the age?" Jesus answered them, "Beware that no one leads you astray. For many will come in my name, saying, 'I am the Messiah!' and they will lead many astray. And you will hear of wars and rumors of wars; see that you are not alarmed; for this must take place, but the end is not yet. For nation will rise against nation, and kingdom against kingdom, and there will be famines and earthquakes in various places: all this is but the beginning of the birth pangs."

Jesus clearly tells us not to be alarmed. He acknowledges that war and famine and natural disasters will be a reality, but he says we are to keep calm by keeping our eyes on God. Paul echoed that same sentiment in Philippians 4:12–13 when he said that he knew what it's like to be well-fed, as well as hungry. He also dared to say he knew the secret to surviving both of those circumstances. What is that secret? I believe we find it in verse 10: "I rejoice in the Lord greatly that now at last you have revived your concern for me; indeed, you were concerned for me, but had no opportunity to show it."

The secret is inner joy.

It's the secret to contentment when we're full, when we're empty, when our bank account looks good, when our bank account looks bad, when the economy is booming, when the economy is sluggish, when we are healthy, when we are ill, when we receive good news, when we receive bad news.

James knew this secret as well. "My brothers and sisters, whenever you face trials of any kind, consider it nothing but joy, because you know that the testing of your faith produces endurance; and let endurance have its full effect, so that you may be mature and complete, lacking in nothing" (James 1:2–4).

Holocaust survivor and author Elie Wiesel wrote about the horrors he witnessed in the concentration camps with his father during World War II. In his book *Night*, Wiesel explained that his father gave him hope during that time so that he could not only survive in the moment but could also build the mental strength to carry on after the persecution. Throughout our lives, we will experience situations that stimulate us to choose either the road of despair or the path of hope. Just as Wiesel prepared mentally to choose hope, I realize there are no stimuli in life in which the hope of God cannot be found.

The reason Paul could be content, whether full or hungry, was that he had the joy of the Lord inside him, which provided him the freedom to trust in God even when he couldn't trust in other humans. Paul's deep joy allowed him to trust the Lord when he couldn't trust the governments of the world. His joy allowed him to trust the Lord when he couldn't trust his own health or his own safety and security. In Nehemiah 8:10, we see that this joy comes from the Lord to fortify us when we face trials: "Then he said to them, 'Go your way, eat the fat and drink sweet wine and send portions of them to those for whom nothing is prepared, for this day is holy to our Lord; and do not be grieved, for the joy of the Lord is your strength.'"

That joy is the very reason Paul was able to say, "I can do all things through him who strengthens me. In any case, it was kind of you to share my distress." It's about doing the work of the Lord in the face of hardship and uncertainty. What I love about this verse is that it emphasizes the shared experience of that hardship and uncertainty. Paul thanked the church at Philippi for sharing in his distress. He didn't bear it alone; his fellow Christians walked alongside him.

My younger sister, my only sibling, is a paramedic in a big city. She worked as a paramedic throughout the entire pandemic. Any risk I had to take as a member of the clergy paled in comparison to the risks she faced daily.

Think about the healthcare workers who, like my sister, put their lives on the line and stepped into the unknown to serve others. They continued to put their lives on the line to serve people who were sick. There was correspondence after correspondence of respiratory therapists, nurses, and doctors begging people to stay home. They said, "If you want to help us, you help us by staying home." Social distancing was the best way we could share in one another's distress by not overburdening the healthcare system any more than it needed. Yet, despite many people who did not accept the advice of healthcare professionals, they patiently and contently served the public through the difficult era of the COVID-19 pandemic.

Nations, businesses, families, and churches will face crises. What makes a crisis manageable is sharing in one another's distress. We are called to soothe one another's nerves, to help one another through the chaos.

Meditations of the Heart

Meditation has been a practice within Christianity since the inception of the faith. Unfortunately, some Christians mistakenly believe that meditation is exclusive to other religions, secular groups, and various schools of thought outside Christianity. This belief is undoubtedly incorrect. It is essential that we re-embrace the power and benefits of a meditative life within the Christian tradition. As people of God, we should not accept the misunderstanding of the concept of meditation, nor should we relinquish it. Meditation is a biblical concept that has to do with the act of being still, practicing solitude, listening to our thoughts, listening to nature, and paying close attention to our consciousness. The Bible encourages us to meditate on God. Psalm 19:14 tells us: "Let the words of my mouth and the meditation of my heart be acceptable to you, O Lord, my rock and my redeemer."

The words we utter, every syllable we pronounce, everything we say—all must be acceptable in the sight of God. How important is this? Jesus himself said that we shall be held accountable for every word we utter (Matt. 12:36). For every careless word, we shall be held accountable, so there should be much thought and care and concern taken with the things we utter.

We have many biblical examples of meditation. Jesus's disciples meditated. Acts 1:13–14 describes how the disciples walked into a room, along with Mary and the brothers of Jesus, and devoted themselves to being a people of prayer.

Here they were in the upper room, the highest place in the building, being still together, being quiet together, being alone together, and praying together. Jesus prayed and meditated in the garden of Gethsemane (Matt. 26:36–46). In Acts 1:13, they were praying in preparation for a mission, to go out into all the ends of the Earth. In Jesus's meditation, he was preparing to fulfill his calling. He sat there, still and quiet, allowing himself to be sifted by God. He wrestled with his inner being. Jesus says, "Father, if it is Your will, take this cup away from Me" (Luke 22:42 NKJV). Yet even in the face of turmoil, he says, "Not My will, but Yours, be done."

Paul exhorted the Romans to be intentional about meditation and transform their minds. In Romans 12:1, he said, "I appeal to you therefore, brothers and sisters, by the mercies of God, to present your bodies as a living sacrifice, holy and acceptable to God." Paul went on to say, "Do not be conformed to this world, but be transformed by the renewing of your minds" (Rom. 12:2).

It's interesting that Paul said the "renewing of *your* minds" (emphasis mine). He is speaking to each of us, making sure we understand that we all must be subject to this kind of self-examination. These aren't just directives for our neighbors or friends or frenemies. They are for each of us, across the board. Paul was not subtle in his encouragement: "I beseech you, I beg you, please, to do this."

Yet, how do we make time for that introspection? It is not easy. I think one of the major problems with our world today is that people are not silent enough, not still enough. As a result, we are not listening to God. We get in the car, and we listen to the radio. We go to our job and listen to our boss, our customers, our students. Then we get back into the car and turn on the radio. We go home, have conversations, and watch a little television. We go to bed, and then we do it all again the next day. Wash. Rinse. Repeat. Nowhere in the day is there any time to just be still and listen. As discussed earlier, we can get so caught up in wanting to be heard that we forget to listen to others.

Let's again think about two people in an argument. Each is so concerned with getting a point across to the other that neither listens to the other. In most cases, their points are aligned, but their communication is the issue. Neither is listening to learn or is asking questions to clarify the other's point. If either was doing this, both would soon learn they are in agreement. Instead, the argument escalates. Far too often, we become so caught up in being heard that we forget to listen. We have to listen to each other. We must also listen to nature.

Listen to nature? Pastor Rodgers, you're getting too far out now.

Yes, listen to nature. It is quite simple. Listen to the wind and to the birds. Appreciate the trees, appreciate the blue skies, appreciate the sunrise and the sunset.

My friend, what are you talking about, appreciate nature?

A part of my personal spiritual growth involves making time to reflect and meditate on nature. I had an opportunity to share this practice with a friend who sought my help with his spiritual journey. He thought it would benefit him to be a part of my spiritual process, to learn by walking in my footsteps, so I invited him to my home one day. It was a beautiful day. I had *A Love Supreme* by John Coltrane playing, and I invited him to sit outside on my back porch, which overlooked my yard and the narrow stream that runs through it. There was a gentle breeze that tenderly kissed each blade of grass, causing the blades to sway eastward and westward, changing the color of the lawn from dark to a lighter shade of green. It was majestic.

The stream flowed vigorously, and the water looked refreshingly inviting. There was not a more perfect day for this exercise.

My friend had a lot on his mind, as he had been house-hunting. He was in the market for a larger home. I instructed him to find something to focus on. "Pick a focal point, and try your best to clear your mind," I told him. "Simply focus. Do this as long as possible until you feel inspiration showering you like a waterfall." We sat in silence while Coltrane played on a loop. After some time, I asked him how he felt, what he felt, what he saw, and what he thought. He said, "I see land and I see a nice house." He had not even been facing my house, and there was none in our direct line of sight. I realized he had not been able to get his mind free of worldly concerns. I found it interesting that he had reduced his meditation to material objects rather than appreciating the testament of nature. It was as if he had forgotten why he had sought my help. I suppose the weight of finding a new home was just too heavy on his mind. The point is that we must make time to clear our minds of temporal objects and make room for the divine. When doing so becomes a struggle, pray about it.

Paul says in Romans 1:20, "For his invisible attributes, namely, his eternal power and divine nature, have been clearly perceived" (ESV). Not partially, not half-heartedly. He says they have been "clearly perceived": ". . . ever since the creation of the world, in the things that have been made. So they are without excuse" (Rom. 1:20 ESV). Paul was referring to the unbelievers. Therefore, we must take time to listen, even to nature.

Listen to the Spirit. Jesus told the disciples, "When the Spirit of truth comes, he will guide you into all the truth, for he will not speak on his own authority, but whatever he hears he will speak, and he will declare to you the things that are to come" (John 16:13 ESV). If the Bible is correct in Acts 2:38 (NIV), where it says, "Repent and be baptized, every one of you . . . . And you will receive the gift of the Holy Spirit," and I truly believe it is, then the Holy Spirit does not lie dormant inside of us. If the Holy Spirit were dormant, there would be no need for the Bible to encourage us by saying, "Do not quench the Spirit" (1 Thess. 5:19). The Spirit should be in us doing a work. The Spirit should be in us doing the sanctifying work, making us holy before God. The Spirit should be in us, whispering to us righteousness and holiness, and if we choose to be still and listen, we might find ourselves being moved toward greatness.

When the disciples sat in the upper room—afraid, scared, and confused, yet preparing to go out to all the ends of the Earth—they were still, they were quiet, and they were prayerful. Why? Over the horizon awaited their task to go out and preach the religion of Jesus, spreading his message across the world. This mission, soon to become outlawed, would lead them to face extreme trials, tribulations, and, ultimately, martyrdom. It was a daunting task, and because of their faithful efforts, the same people who were persecuting them converted and started to promote them. They were destined for greatness. So, before they headed out, they took the time to be still, to be quiet, and to listen.

We see that same faithfulness in Jesus in the garden of Gethsemane. Greatness was upon the horizon. He was about to do the work to save the world from its transgressions, to be beaten brutally, to be shamed, killed, and to rise again. Knowing what lay ahead, Jesus took time to be silent, to be still, and to listen.

Once we are able to do this, we can truly examine ourselves by asking crucial questions. *What is it that I really want?* That question is so important because inside that question lies our motives. *Why is it that we do what we do? Why is it that we say what we say?* Ask these questions, and then take time to wrestle with them, allowing the light inside you to cast out the darkness. If we never take time to be still and listen, then we can never examine ourselves and understand who we are and who we have the potential to become.

The oft-repeated saying of Captain von Trapp from *The Sound of Music*, "Activity suggests a life filled with purpose," is either complete sarcasm or completely fallacious. The myth of busyness is destroying us and corroding our society. We have tried to make busyness a noble ethic, but I would argue that it falls far short. There's nothing wrong with being a little busy, but busyness to the point where our children miss us, our church family misses us, God misses us, or we even miss ourselves is not physically or spiritually healthy. The idea that this degree of busyness is noble is a lie. In the Bible, we find countless examples of God's people preparing for their greatness by being still.

Many of us want to be great, but before we can launch into that greatness, we have to take time for Shabbat—a regular rhythm of rest, silence, solitude, prayer, and self-reflection. Creating regular spaces like this increases our capacity to remember that everything we have comes from the Lord. It shapes our soul to become patient and increasingly curious about everything God is doing in the world around us.

Reflection Questions

- "I can do all things through him who strengthens me" (Phil. 4:13 ESV). Think about all the responsibilities baked into these words. Are they words we pray only when we seek the

Lord's blessing upon our will and desire, or can we confidently pray these words in surrender to God's will?

▶ Describe a time when you were aware of being at God's mercy and fully prepared to accept his will. How did you prepare for the outcome? What did you learn about yourself? About God? What will you do in the future to prepare yourself so that God's will be done?

▶ Think about the pact we are making with God every time we pray the Lord's Prayer: "Thy will be done" (Matt. 6:10 KJV). Think about times when we chose our will over God's will. None of us is perfect. Meditate on this pact. What are some habits we can form to remain open to God's will?

▶ We all seek purpose in life, but sometimes we confuse purpose with busyness. Take inventory of your activities in a typical day. Then review the list to determine which activities are necessary to survival, which serve God, and which are time passers. Pray for discernment and the strength to make good use of time, including time to be still, to meditate, and to grow in faith.

4

COMMUNITY

"Sticks and stones may break my bones, but words will never hurt me." While that mantra serves as protective armor for receiving messages, it should also be at top of mind every time we deliver a message, along with the saying, "Think before you speak." Words can hurt. Words can cause emotional and spiritual injury when they tear down rather than build up another. Words can affect people's lives. The tongue is powerful. The tongue has the power to speak life or death into existence.

During the COVID-19 pandemic, we faced times of increased physical distancing. Due to communications being reduced to Zoom, FaceTime, and Google Meet, we were using our tongues, verbal communication, more than normal. The right set of words spoken the wrong way has the potential to lead to an explosion, which we may have experienced. That is why we must be ever so careful to season our words with salt and to tame our tongues. I appreciate what the writer says in James 3:2–12:

For all of us make many mistakes. Anyone who makes no mistakes in speaking is perfect, able to keep the whole body in check with a bridle. If we put bits into the mouths of horses to make them obey us, we guide their whole bodies. Or look at ships: though they are so large that it takes strong winds to drive them, yet they are guided by a very small rudder wherever the will of the pilot directs. So also the tongue is a small member, yet it boasts of great exploits.

How great a forest is set ablaze by a small fire! And the tongue is a fire. The tongue is placed among our members as a world of iniquity; it stains the whole body, sets on fire the cycle of nature, and is itself set on fire by hell. For every species of beast and bird, of reptile and sea creature, can be tamed and has been tamed by the human species, but no one can tame the tongue—a restless evil, full of deadly poison.

With it we bless the Lord and Father, and with it we curse those who are made in the likeness of God. From the same mouth come blessing and cursing. My brothers and sisters, this ought not to be so. Does a spring pour forth from the same opening both fresh and brackish water? Can a fig tree, my brothers and sisters, yield olives, or a grapevine figs? No more can salt water yield fresh.

At the XIII International AIDS Conference in July 2000, former South African president Nelson Mandela said, "It is never my custom to use words lightly. If twenty-seven years in prison have done anything to us, it was to use the silence of solitude to make us understand how precious words are and how real speech is in its impact on the way people live and die."[1] We must speak life to one another.

There are words that build life and words that lead to death. For example, if someone shares with me their desire to write a book, I can respond with, "That sounds like a great idea. Tell me more." That response would be encouraging. We have to be careful to not project negativity onto people, which we often do inadvertently. If I responded negatively, I would be speaking death to that person. Such responses could look like these: "Why would you want to do that?" "Don't you know no one reads books anymore?" "Do you even know where to start?" Often we respond through our own lens colored by our frame of reference and fears, and we project that onto others. Language like this kills a person's spirit and dreams, which could ultimately lead to physical death if that person gives up on the inherent quest to find his or her best iteration of life.

Let's take the hypothetical book-writing example further. We'll call the person John. Let's say I know that John does not have the talent to write a book. I might feel compelled to break the bad news to him, thinking I'm doing him a favor. If so, I would still break his spirit, which in the end would not be good. There is another way around this, especially if John is visibly filled with enthusiasm about his idea. I could match his enthusiasm, ask about the book, and wish him well. I could show empathy and congratulate him for taking on such an arduous task. With that, I could encourage him and tell him that writers often put together a team of coauthors, coaches, researchers, editors, and others to help move projects like this along.

This is how we speak life into another. The challenge is getting into the habit of doing so. A lot of us are unconsciously in the habit of speaking death. Perhaps that's because we have not accomplished our dreams, or because others have always spoken death into us. Perhaps our lives are stagnant, and we simply cannot comprehend or bear to see others progress to the next chapter in their lives. Subconsciously, we speak death into others when we perceive they will achieve more than we have achieved. As bad as that example is, there are worse examples yet of speaking death into someone.

The Power of Words to Destroy

Some people spread lies, gossip, and rumors about others that could be dangerous. Let's use this hypothetical example of two coworkers, a man and a woman. We'll call them Harry and Sue. Each is married. Because they work on several projects together, they are often seen together in each other's offices, the lunchroom, or the conference room. Sometimes they have to work late to meet deadlines. Their spouses are understanding and supportive. Now, suppose someone in the office begins to question Harry and Sue's work relationship, suggesting they are having an affair. That rumor could reach one of the spouses and destroy that couple's relationship. Taken to the extreme, the thought of infidelity could lead to any number of bad things, including revenge and, ultimately, physical harm. Rumors can spin out of control.

Nosiness or outright deliberate lies are another form of speaking death. I saw a news report about unnecessary police calls on African Americans. The example given involved a few men repairing a neighbor's car. Someone called the police and suggested that the men were up to no good. For African American men in this age, such a call could end up disastrously. Imagine the potential chaos that could ensue if multiple cop cars pulled up with blaring sirens and blazing lights.

James 3:1–12 addresses the taming of the tongue. Think about the power of positivity we possess. The power to do God's will. The power to make a difference, to bring others to Christ, simply by thinking before we speak.

Words are like seeds. We must think about what we are planting with our language. We can plant something that will be nutritious, that will give life, or we can plant something that will lead to sin and condemnation. What seeds are we planting all around us? Are we planting seeds that will bring forth a beautiful garden, or are we planting seeds of toxicity and harm?

Words are like fire. They can generate warmth and comfort. They can warm an entire home, purify, and clean. Like fire, however, if not regulated or used properly, words can cause great harm. They can set an entire home ablaze.

Words are like wind. They can be as soothing as a gentle breeze on a warm summer day or as ferocious as a tornado, destroying everything in their path.

Words are also like water. They can be cleansing, refreshing, and life-giving, keeping us hydrated and healthy. Like a tidal wave, words can also crash down upon us, overwhelming us and instantly wiping out our motivation, drowning us in a cesspool of negativity.

Language is complicated. It is important that we choose our words with the utmost care. As Christians, followers of Jesus, we must always be aware of this responsibility. If we destroy a person's spirit with harsh or careless words, we can destroy their desire to serve God or their neighbors. We could hurt their relationship with God as well as our own relationship with God.

Jesus said, "It would be better to be thrown into the sea with a millstone hung around your neck than to cause one of these little ones to fall into sin" (Luke 17:2 NLT). Using words that are not productive is dangerous business. In fact, Matthew 12:36–37 quotes Jesus instructing, "I tell you, on the day of judgment you will have to give an account for every careless word you utter; for by your words, you will be justified, and by your words you will be condemned."

While we may never know, it seems author and motivational speaker Dale Carnegie was influenced by that passage in Matthew when he wrote in his timeless classic *How to Win Friends & Influence People*: "Never criticize, condemn, or complain. Any fool can criticize, and most fools do." Putting that advice into practice requires a bit of work, and it can be done. We simply have to form good habits. In addition to thinking before we speak, remember the old adage, "If you have nothing nice to say, say nothing at all." For some, remaining quiet comes naturally. For others, just the opposite is true. When we feel compelled to speak, for whatever reason, we should begin with a positive comment rather than blurt out the first thing that comes to mind. Saying something nice sets a positive tone, makes others feel good, and makes us look good in the process, as long as we are authentic.

Being mindful of our speech is not just about avoiding mean words; it's also about not using irresponsible words, such as words that put money over humanity. Some people do not care about other humans as much as they do their bank accounts. They are focused on one thing, as The O'Jays sang, ". . . that mean, mean, mean, mean, mean green."[2] That is, they care about money above all else. Many people only care about money and making more money and how to get to the bottom line.

Some will use words to indoctrinate, to condition, or to brainwash others simply to uphold their agenda of making more money. Some don't care if they pollute the oceans and the skies and air. They don't care if they make people sick. They don't care if they cause birth defects. They don't care if they destroy the Earth as long as it increases their bank account.

Words can be used to favor men over women, to injure women, and to subjugate women. Words can be used to treat men poorly as well. People can treat men poorly and not treat them according to how God would want them to be treated. Words can also be used to promote racial hatred. Words can be used to make people think poorly or negatively about certain races and certain individuals and certain ethnic groups. Folks who do this will be held accountable for this in the last days.

Words can be used to teach the young generation to be selfish instead of being righteous for God. Why do people want to do that? Why do some people want to promote selfishness among generations of young people? Why does there seem to be a desire to remove God from the public square? Could it be because a generation that rises up and says, "I care about the whole more than I care about my own wants," will be a generation that changes the world? Could it be that a generation that rises up and says, "I care about the needs of the whole instead of my own wants," will be a generation that revolutionizes society? Do some fear a society that is more aligned with who God wants us to be?

Society will not change until we learn that we are all interconnected and until we act accordingly, caring authentically for one another. It is not possible to be completely isolated from other humans, and so it is necessary to care about human dignity and protect the personhood of all. We must take heed and think before we speak to one another individually, as a group, and as leaders and policymakers. Words matter! Are our words full of care? Are the words we use full of selfishness? Are the words we use seasoned with hate? Are our words chosen to fulfill a personal agenda only? Are our words shaped by our own anxieties, selfish ambitions, hastiness? Jesus tells us to choose our words carefully. If we are not careful with our words, we will be condemned.

The Beauty of a Word Well-Spoken

Being conscious of our speech is about more than avoiding mean words and irresponsible language. Casual, careless words can be dangerous, too. In Colossians 4:6, the Bible says, "Let your speech always be gracious, seasoned with salt, so that you may know how you ought to answer everyone." Food can be a real joy, but food cooked without seasoning can be unpleasant. You might not want to eat it.

A family friend from my youth had the reputation for being a subpar cook. When she brought food to a gathering, no one wanted to eat it. It was not seasoned well and was always very bland. She always took home a dish full of whatever she brought to any occasion. God bless her heart. We appreciated the effort, though. Bland words have a similar effect. They get ignored.

When we season our words with wisdom, patience, and love, the people we are trying to reach are more likely to hear what we are trying to say. When it seems no one wants to listen to us, we have to consider the manner in which we relay our messages, the tone we use, and certainly the words we choose. These things combined have an emotional impact, and as Maya Angelou famously said, "At the end of the day, people won't remember what you said or did, they will remember how you made them feel."

Consider the following:

- It is as easy to offer someone a piece of gum or a mint as it is to say, "Your breath stinks!"
- When we haven't heard from someone in a while, rather than assume that person is harboring a grudge

against us, perhaps we need to check in to see if he or she is okay. Could the person have had an emergency or some sort of mishap?
- Assume positive intentions on the part of others. Avoid making assumptions. Seek first to understand.
- "Are you okay?" "You've been in my thoughts." "How can I be there for you?" "Help me to understand." These are the kinds of words we all need to hear and the kinds of words we need to be sharing with one another.

I realize we live in a turbulent time and that there will be conflicts. I get that, but even amid conflict, there is a way to communicate using words seasoned with care and love. "You know what? I struggle to understand your decision. Can you help me understand?"

Here's another one: "I am hopeful that we can find a solution to this. Can we work together to find that solution?"

How about this one: "I don't think I came across the way I'd like. Can you give me a chance to further explain?"

The tongue can do many things. Just with the utterance of mere words, the tongue can cause a person to lose their life. If we talk to a very fragile person at the wrong time, the words we use could cause that person to possibly want to harm himself and maybe even end his life—just because of the way we spoke to him. The way we communicate things to people can make them lose hope in themselves. It could cause them to feel so low that it could take years to recover.

The tongue can do great, great harm. The writer in James is right about what he says regarding the tongue, but the tongue can do some very positive things, too. The tongue can be used to save lives, to speak peace into the world, to be an instrument of shalom and hope. That's what the tongue can do. The tongue can protect and comfort someone. We may have someone approach us full of anger and rage, and in that moment, we have an opportunity to defuse that person, to show him or her an alternative to violence and destruction that could cause harm.

Our tongues can say, "Well, let me go along with their anger," and cause that person to do some harm to somebody else. No, don't do that. We need to use our words to protect each other. What the angry person is saying could be a cry for help. We can use our tongues to respond: "Hold on. Be strong. Help is coming." The tongue can be used to pray for somebody. The tongue can be used to bring comfort on rainy days. The tongue can be used to heal. May our tongues never be used to destroy.

Refer to this chapter for help with how to best use the tongue. Let us consider how to make sure we are ever so careful with our words, with our tongues. May we speak life into one another and never speak death.

Staying on the Boat

When I was taught, as a child, the story of Jesus and Peter walking on the water (Matt. 14:22–33), the emphasis was almost always placed on Peter and the faith he had to get out of the boat. Peter had faith to walk on the water. Some went as far as to say that Peter was somehow better than those disciples who stayed in the boat. I want to offer an alternate interpretation of this story.

When I was in my twenties, completing my undergraduate degree, I worked as a deckhand on a cruise ship. It was a difficult job. One day, I was working on one of the smaller boats, which was empty. The captain said we had to reach our destination faster. We were headed into deeper water. A storm whipped up, and soon our boat was being tossed around like a small toy. We walked on deck at a forty-five-degree angle. At least that's what it felt like. Before I knew it, I got very sick. I could feel my face turning green. I had not turned green, at least as far as I know, but I was seasick and it was terrible.

After finding the first mate—a guy who was a little bit off the chain—I asked him, "Help me, please. Do you have some Dramamine? Do you have something? I'm very seasick."

He answered, "No. I don't have any Dramamine, but I do have something that can help you." After he opened the door to the deck, he showed me the swirling ocean with its bashing waves. He said, "If you jump into the water, you will immediately feel better." I tell you the truth—if I'd seen Jesus out there, I would have jumped into that water. No question. That's how bad I felt. My point is that sometimes it takes more faith to stay in the boat. Consider the Bible story again. Peter volunteered to get up and out of the boat. Jesus granted that permission. When he got out of the boat, he wasn't ready for what was out there, but he had faith in Christ. In my situation, as bad as I felt, my deck mate showed me that I could be worse off still. There are times when staying the course requires just as much faith.

Staying in the boat requires commitment and strength. It requires us to be long-suffering. It is the very act of having patience. Staying in the boat requires faith that God can use you in the most challenging circumstances and that God can bring you through the most difficult situations. I think about those three Jewish men—Shadrach, Meshach, Abednego—who were threatened by King Nebuchadnezzar. They knew they faced a fiery furnace for refusing to worship his golden statue, but they stood their ground, proclaiming that they would not worship any false gods and that their God had the power to save them from the blazing fire. Their defiant words are inspiring even today:

> O Nebuchadnezzar, we have no need to present a defense to you in this matter. If our God whom we serve is able to deliver us from the furnace of blazing fire and out of your hand, O king, let him deliver us. But if not, be it known to you, O king, that we will not serve your gods and we will not worship the golden statue that you have set up. (Dan. 3:16–18)

This kind of action—staying right where you are and continuing to do what you believe is right—requires tremendous faith. Think about your life. Do you have the faith required to stay in the boat? Are you willing to weather the storms that might come up in your relationships? Are you willing to weather the storms that might affect the institutions in which you participate? Or when trouble comes, will you jump out of the boat?

Some people hop from church to church during their lives, and they are some of the most critical and nitpicky Christians around. They often contribute little to the maintenance of the church or toward the encouragement of their sisters and brothers. Tough times come and go, but tough people don't. In times of challenge and struggle, it's important to remember that sometimes the most faithful thing we can do is stay on the boat. Stay put, and trust that Jesus is going to take care of us in that boat.

Staying on the boat provides an opportunity to affect the trajectory of the journey. Staying on the boat provides an opportunity to be involved in the future of the voyage. Staying on the boat provides an opportunity to take up an oar and steer the ship in the direction God wants. Staying in the boat means God can use us to heal relationships among our shipmates. Staying on the boat, however, requires faith, perseverance, and obedience.

We might pray, "Lord, Lord, help me find another church and get out of my current one." Then the Lord does this, but we find the same thing in the new church that we disliked in the former one. Sometimes, the problem is not around us but is in us. God will provide us with the same lesson over and over until we learn it. If we would have stayed in the boat and listened, God would have helped us weather the storm, and through the process, transform us and the church environment.

Likewise, some folks jump from job to job to job, praying, "Lord, give me another job where I can be blessed. Lord, give me another job that can solve my problems." God might allow us to move, just like Jesus allowed Peter to get out of the boat, but we might jump ship only to experience fierce winds and crashing waves. Then we realize we should have remained in the boat.

Consider the marriage boat. Studies show that economic issues are among the top ten issues that lead married couples to divorce.[3] While financial struggles can be a catalyst to many other issues, far too many couples choose to abandon ship at the first sign of a storm. While no one should remain in an abusive situation, the divorce rate in the United States is evidence that many people need restored faith. They need to open their hearts and minds to God. Marriage is worth fighting for. Even though relationships can be tumultuous, and the storm may make us seasick at times, we must place our faith in God. It is vital that we place our very marriages in God's healing hands.

Let's consider friendships. Are we willing to stay in the friendship boat or cast aside a friendship at the first sign of disagreement? *I ain't talking to him no more. I ain't talking to her no more. I'm done with him. Do you know what he said to me? Do you know what he did to me?* "I'm jumping out of the boat. I'm sick of these folks on this boat, so I'm coming out,"[4] like

Diana Ross sings in her 1980 hit song. But sometimes staying in the boat and letting God use us to restore those relationships is the true act of faith and selflessness.

It's not easy. Many people on the boat with us are intense, selfish, and just plain annoying. I imagine Peter had the same complaints. Can't you just hear him? *Andrew is always sharing fishing stories, exaggerating his catches. James and John, the sons of thunder, are always arguing over who is the greatest. Thomas demands proof of everything, and Judas is always asking for spare coins. I don't know why he needs so much money. They're all crazy!*

Then in comes Jesus with his rebuke: *Peter, who are you to say all of this about them? Do we need to talk about you, Peter? Shall we go down the list, Peter, since you want to talk bad about Andrew and the sons of thunder? You, who wanted to keep fishing when you first met me; you, who tried to convince me not to fulfill my purpose, and I had to tell you, "Get behind me, Satan!"* [Matt. 16:23]. *You, who are swift to anger and chop off a man's ear. You, who talk trash, but when it's time to show up, you run and hide until the rooster crows. Peter, are you so quick to get out of the boat because you have not yet examined yourself?*

So often we cannot recognize our own problematic tendencies. We cannot recognize how we contribute to the dysfunction. We cannot recognize how we play a part in the story, and we end up getting out of the boat. And guess what happens? The faith we lacked while we were in the boat is the same lack of faith that causes us to sink outside of the boat.

Take heart, though. Jesus chose the imperfect Peter, the imperfect James, the imperfect John, the imperfect Matthew, and the imperfect Bartholomew. Jesus's friends were a motley crew of broken individuals just like us. Like Jesus called his first disciples, he calls us. In Matthew 4:19, Jesus tells Simon Peter and Andrew that he will make them fishers of men. A saying inspired by this verse reads, "Be ye fishers of men! You catch them and he'll clean them."

We need to realize our own dysfunction. We have all sinned and come short of the glory of God. We need to realize our own contribution to situations. We may dislike hearing this, but we must learn to love the ministry of restoration and repairing. We must trust God to work in us and allow God to work through us. If we jump out too soon, we risk missing a blessing, and the people we left on board might miss a blessing as a result.

We might be tired, but we must stay in the boat. We might be frustrated. We might be discouraged. Stay in the boat and watch Jesus transform our circumstances, and we will say, "It's true. You are the Son of God" (Matt. 16:16).

Reflection Questions

- ▶ Negative talk comes from a negative mindset, and most times we do not even realize our minds are set to the negative. Pay attention to your thought process. Be honest with yourself. Do you tend to face most situations from a negative or positive point of view? What expectations do you have ahead of any conversation or any routine activity like driving to work? Do you anticipate the worst or the best?

- ▶ What are some ways you can get into the habit of positive self-talk?

- ► Consider a conversation when you unintentionally hurt someone with your words. If you had the opportunity to relive that moment, what would you do differently?

- ► Consider a conversation when you were hurt by someone else's words. How did you react? Did you internalize the conversation, feeling bad about yourself? Did you think poorly of the other person, hold a grudge, or find compassion for that person?

- ► As fallen humans, we tend to take God's will and bring it down to our level of understanding rather than completely giving our lives over in trust. In what areas of your life do you struggle to let go and let God?

- ► What is one concern you can commit to handing over to God today? If you prefer to be in control or struggle with trust, pray for perseverance, strength, and wisdom.

Notes

[1] Nelson Mandela, "Closing Address at the 13th International AIDS Conference, Durban," July 14, 2000, http://www.mandela.gov.za/mandela_speeches/2000/000714_aidsconf.htm.

[2] The O'Jays, "For the Love of Money," by Kenneth Gamble, Leon Huff, and Anthony Jackson, track 1 on side 2, *Ship Ahoy*, Sigma Sound Studios, 1973.

[3] Hope Gillette, "The Top 12 Reasons for Divorce," PsychCentral, October 25, 2022, https://psychcentral.com/relationships/top-reasons-for-divorce.

[4] Diana Ross, "I'm Coming Out," written by Bernard Edwards and Nile Rodgers, track 4 on side A, *Diana*, Power Station, 1980.

5

FAITH AND CONVICTION

What is faith? Sometimes, when I ask, "What is faith?" someone will quickly recite Hebrews 11:1: "Now faith is the assurance of things hoped for, the conviction of things not seen." I say, "Oh, that's great, but what does that mean?" Then we start to wonder.

What is faith, this concept that is so important to our Christian walk? Notice I said our Christian walk, not our Christian talk. One might say a pivotal scripture in Christianity is Romans 1:17, which says, "The just shall live by faith" (KJV). The justified shall live by faith. Those of us who have been washed in the blood of Christ have become justified, or made right.

We know immediately by reading this text that faith is something we live. It's not just something we feel. We don't only feel faith. Faith is not something we just think about. It comes outside of our minds. Faith is something we do as well. Faith affects how we make our decisions. Faith affects our spirituality. Faith makes us courageous. Faith makes us fearless.

We can know what's right as rain, what's right as day, but because in some way it's impractical, we won't do it. Faith makes us fearless in those moments. Faith affects us.

The God we love, the God we praise, the God where we find our absolute truth and objective authority is also a God we have never seen. Yet, in this God, we find our conviction. About what, exactly, are we convicted?

Conviction is typically followed by action. When a judge or jury convicts a person, it's followed by a sentence. When our friends convict us, they force us to see the error of our ways. It makes us want to change. When God is our conviction, we give ourselves up completely to him and to his plan. We give ourselves away so that God might use us. The concept of being used generally has a negative connotation. No one wants to be exploited by others, especially in a manner that offends our dignity. When we are sought after for our talents and gifts, our dignity is affirmed. Thus, being used in this manner is welcomed because we feel respected and appreciated. When we lend our gifts to the greater good, we feel a sense of pride.

Such was the case for the heroic men of the 121st Engineer Combat Battalion during World War II. Each had a clear sense of purpose when he landed on Omaha beach with the first US forces. The role of the battalion was to charge forward under heavy machine gun fire to clear the field of mines so the forces behind them could storm the beaches of Normandy. Battalion soldiers were being used in a manner that was bigger than themselves. They likely had no idea that history would revere them with the utmost honor. They were focused on their mission to protect freedom. Likewise, when we allow ourselves to be used by God, we are committing to the greater good—what is best for our fellow human, what is best for us as individuals, what is best for the planet, and what is the best use of our

God-given gifts. With this perspective, many of us are eager to be used by God.

Similarly, this desire to use our gifts for the greater good keeps us motivated in our daily vocation. We don our best when we interview for a job or present our skills and experiences on a résumé. We speak articulately when vying for the favor of an employer with whom we wish to work, whose mission we hope to carry out. This requires trust and faith that God will use us in a substantive way, but for that to happen, we must die unto self and live for God. We must question whether we have this type of deep faith. We must pray for this type of faith. It is the only real faith to have. When Jesus said, "Take up [your] cross and follow me" (Matt. 16:24), he was calling us to this type of uncompromising faith.

Faith always believes before it sees. Imagine a long staircase. You don't know what lies at the top. You're told something wonderful is at the top. Every step you take on this staircase is an act of faith, which means that for a person who makes every decision based on what they can hear, based on what they can taste, based on what they can see, faith might not make any sense at all.

The thought of living by faith might be lunacy to some because it only makes sense for them to live by what they can see and what is tangible. Consider 1 Corinthians 1:18, where Paul writes that the gospel is foolishness to those who are perishing. No one truthfully lives by sight alone. No one does this. Am I right about that? Think about it. When we eat someone's cooking but didn't watch him prepare it, we are participating in an act of faith. We have faith that the person didn't poison the food. We have faith that the person didn't spit in the food. We have faith that the person wasn't digging in the garden before going into the house to cook our food without washing his hands. We simply sit and we eat.

Driving on the road requires an act of faith. First, we have faith our own vehicle is going to function properly, and if we aren't driving, we have faith that the person driving will drive like they have some sense. Even if we are driving, we have some faith that the drivers to our left and our right will drive like they have sense. When we get on an airplane, we don't know if the pilot is sober or if the mechanic took any shortcuts. It's an act of faith.

When we have surgery, we allow someone with a paper from a university to administer medicine that makes us go to sleep, so deeply asleep that they cut us and we don't wake up. They go inside our bodies with tiny tools, and when we wake up, we say, "Thank you." That's an act of faith. When we sit in a chair, we have faith that the legs will not break. When we drive in a parking garage or over a bridge, we have faith that the structure will not collapse.

People who think they make all their decisions based on what they see fail to realize they walk by faith, too. They're just afraid to admit it, or they never really thought deeply about it. Their faith might be in numbers and statistics, their faith might be in the odds, their faith might be in humans, but they are practicing an act of faith. I think genuine Christians are honest about faith because they recognize the beauty of God's creation, a world made so perfectly for human life, which was confirmed by the life of Christ. The planet on which we live is just the right distance from the sun, not too close and not too far away. The Earth has the perfect atmosphere, just the right amount of gravitational pull. Everything on Earth is perfect for human survival.

I think Christians observe creation and realize, "This is something that is masterful. It can only be created by a masterful creator." We say we want to submit ourselves to the creator who has revealed himself through creation, but also through the Word of God and also through the Son, Christ Jesus. I think Christians are honest about faith because we realize everything we do, such as performing surgery on another, is only by the grace of God.

If a chef has the ability to cook a meal and lay it before me, it is only by the grace of God that she can do so. If a pilot can fly a plane and it can take off in the sky like an osprey and land like a seagull, it's only by the grace of God that this happens. I think Christians are honest about faith because we realize the principle of first cause. We realize that everything has come together as the result of something bigger than us, something absolute that has put together the whole entire universe, something that is eternal and not finite.

Hebrews 11:1 concludes with "the conviction of things not seen" (ESV). It was that conviction that led Abraham to leave home and walk out into an endless desert. When Abraham walked out into that desert and looked to the north, looked to the east, looked to the south, and then looked to the west, all he saw was desert, and he had to walk in faith with God.

The same thing happened to the Hebrew people during the exodus, and they struggled with it, but while they were walking, they were walking in faith with God. Going way back, it was conviction that caused Abel to give the more perfect offering. It was conviction that caused Moses's parents to have the good sense to hide him from the persecution of Pharaoh. It was conviction that caused the Hebrew midwives to hide the other Hebrew babies during the same time. It was conviction that caused Rahab to protect the Hebrew spies who came to her house.

What does our faith convict us to do? We learn from Hebrews 11:1–2 that if we have faith, we are going to have a conviction. That conviction is going to move us to do something, and what we are doing is not a part of our plan; it's a part of God's plan. When we read through Hebrews 11, we find people who were convicted by their faith, and their conviction moved them to do something great for God. What has your faith convicted you to do? How has your faith invited you into God's plan? Despite your mistakes, despite your shortcomings, despite your weaknesses, despite all this stuff that makes you human, how is God using you? Because being used by God is a part of our faith, faith is more than what is just sitting dormant in our hearts. Faith flows out of our hearts, into our hands, and then into our deeds.

Our faith is connected to why we were created: for good works. In Ephesians 2:8–10, Paul declares that we have been saved through faith and not by ourselves: "It is the gift of God—not the result of works, so that no one may boast." According to Scripture, our faith flows from our heart to our hands and becomes a part of us. It is a part of who we are and a part of our life.

As Romans 1:17 says, we shall "live by faith." Of course, carrying out God's instruction to live by faith is challenging, which is why we lean on each other. As humans, we are wired toward communion with one another. This is God's design. We come to the assembly so our faith can be encouraged. We come to the assembly so our faith can be made strong and can remain strong. We come to the assembly so our faith can be prodded and formed. If we doubt the assembly is important to faith, we should speak with someone who has fallen away from God and the assembly and then returned. Ask about that journey. Why did that person stray? What happened during the "down" time? We can refer to it as down time because we know true contentment is not attainable without God. What prompted the person to return? Was it a major epiphany or a series of subtle signs that led the person to realize something was amiss?

The assembly is important. We assemble to lift up one another because God has a plan for each of us. Encouraging one another is a part of God's plan. We encourage one another as we come together to assemble, and this is a part of God's plan. I would be dishonest, however, if I said that practicing the conviction of faith is only about coming to the assembly. Coming to the assembly is an essential component of our faith practice, but it's not the only part.

James 2:14–26 teaches us that faith and works go hand in hand, and the good works we do take place not only on Sunday morning, but they also should be a way of life, as stated in Ephesians. So, the question I pose at this moment is: What does our faith make us do? What does our faith stir in us that inspires us to act? Faith stirs us to something we know we must accomplish, something in which we feel compelled to participate, in which we know we must be involved.

Belief pushes us to do something. Belief that they could fly pushed the Wright brothers to invent the airplane. If they hadn't had that belief, they never would have invented the plane and flown it at Kitty Hawk on the Outer Banks of North Carolina, my home state.

When a man loves a woman, he doesn't say, "Hey, I believe I love you," and stop there without further action. Otherwise, she might never truly believe that he loves her. If he says it with his lips, it should show in his actions and his deeds. It's the same with faith. Faith is not something that just stays in the heart.

Faith flows out through our deeds. It's how we live our lives and bear witness to God's grace.

When a man named Martin Cooper invented the cell phone, he believed it first. He believed it was possible. It was a radical idea to envision a phone with no wires attached, and he pushed it through its development.

Belief never just stays in the heart. It flows out through our actions. Again, consider what actions are inspired by our faith in God. What has faith in God caused us to do? Every way we answer that question should boil down to one word, and that word we can find in Romans 1 in the second half of verse 4 through the first half of verse 5: "Jesus Christ our Lord, through whom we have received grace and apostleship to bring about the obedience of faith."

Every way we answer the question "What does my faith make me do?" should begin and end with *obey*. Obey the will of God, the whole will of God—not just what I want to hear, not just what I want to do, but everything God wants me to do. Pray these words from Romans 16:26–27: "but is now disclosed, and through the prophetic writings is made known to all the Gentiles, according to the command of the eternal God, to bring about the obedience of faith—to the only wise God, through Jesus Christ, to whom be the glory forever! Amen."

Throughout Hebrews 11, we encounter characters who obeyed the will of God. They allowed their faith to make them do something, and because of that, they were obedient to faith. Their faith was in God. What has our faith made us do? Prayerfully, the answer is obedience—obedience to everything God has told us to do. The true sign of faith is obedience to God in every way. Jesus is a primary example of being obedient to the point of death. Likewise, John the Baptist was obedient to the point of a horrific death, as were the apostles. There are examples of obedience throughout the Bible: Abraham's obedience to sacrifice his son Isaac, Noah's obedience to build an ark ahead of the great flood, Daniel's refusal to eat the king's meat or drink his wine, Joseph's obedience to take Mary as his wife and his obedience to flee to Egypt with Mary and Jesus, and so on.

Has our faith convicted us? Yes, obedience is assembling with the saints on the first day of the week, which is when we gather. Yes, obedience is loving our neighbors as ourselves, which also bleeds into acts of compassion individually and socially. Yes, obedience is encouraging our brothers and sisters in the faith. Yes, obedience is walking in God's unique calling for us.

Heeding God's calling is not always easy, but it is always possible. I did not recognize it at the time, but my ministry discernment began when I was sixteen. I delivered my first sermon in a small church in Kinston, North Carolina. The church was big that day because we were celebrating an area-wide fellowship, where people from neighboring churches gathered together at one location. I stuttered and stammered through the sermon, but overall, it was good, especially given my age. After the service, many people approached me and told me that I should consider preaching. I shrugged off their comments. When I was a high school student, I did not feel impelled to consider such a high calling, although it did pique my interest.

Upon graduating high school, I joined the Air Force. While serving, I developed a reputation for offering intercessory prayers. People came to me and requested my prayers about all sorts of things. Word quickly spread that the prayers of those who prayed with me were answered. My fellow servicemen nicknamed me "Rev."

Following an injury, I was sent to medical holding for a time. While there, I read the Bible cover to cover at least four times. We were only permitted to bring one book, and it had to be religious in nature. The stoic rule seemed to align with the character of the building; it was a no-frills, sterile white building with cement blocks.

My deep dive into the Bible led me to launch a Bible study group, and it grew legs. Our barracks contained what was called a Protestant church, but there were other churches on the base. The church I attended, although Protestant, was unlike the larger, more popular Protestant church. It had no music or video screens, and it enforced the bootcamp rule prohibiting fraternization. Nevertheless, many bypassed the larger church to worship and study the Bible with me. This was a big feat.

Noto, a man in our Bible study, approached me about being baptized. He wanted to accept Jesus Christ into his heart and wanted me to baptize him. Although I was honored and excited, I was hesitant, so I took Noto to the base and asked the chaplain, who ministered at the large church, if I could baptize him. Without giving the chaplain an opportunity to answer, I immediately became apologetic, saying that I accepted that this would not be possible but that I thought it was important that Noto be baptized. I was talking my way out of it. To my surprise, the chaplain said, "Oh, no. You most certainly can baptize Noto."

As I baptized Noto, I felt the Holy Spirit move me. It was a feeling I had never experienced. I knew at that moment that I was called to be a minister. I immediately wrote to my parents to tell them. Accepting our respective callings is not always difficult, but living them can be. This life is filled with challenges.

Ministers, like other leaders, often don a happy face, but like the song "The Tears of a Clown" says, the smile is "only there trying to fool the public."[1] Ministry can be rough. We get beaten up by the world and sometimes by our very own churches. The weight of scrutiny is a lot to bear. I bet if we polled a hundred ministers, privately asking them what advice they'd give their younger selves during that period of discernment, many would advise against entering the ministry, but they may not admit that publicly. If I had a time machine and could go back and consult my younger self, I certainly would have trouble convincing young Lawrence to heed the call to ministry, but I would not dissuade him. Instead, I'd share some learned experiences about which to be wary and encourage him to move forward for two reasons. Two Scripture passages come to mind when I think about a religious calling: Romans 8:18 and 1 Peter 4:13.

"I consider that the sufferings of this present time are as nothing compared with the glory to be revealed for us" (Rom. 8:18 NABRE). We Christians sometimes expect that there will be no suffering in this day and age, but the truth is there will be suffering, challenges, and hardships. Paul experienced very difficult times.

> Five times at the hands of the Jews I received forty lashes minus one. Three times I was beaten with rods, once I was stoned, three times I was shipwrecked, I passed a night and a day on the deep; on frequent journeys, in dangers from rivers, dangers from robbers, dangers from my own race, dangers from Gentiles, dangers in the city, dangers in the wilderness, dangers at sea, dangers among false brothers; in toil and hardship, through many sleepless nights, through hunger and thirst, through frequent fastings, through cold and exposure. And apart from these things, there is the daily pressure upon me of my anxiety for all the churches. Who is weak, and I am not weak? Who is led to sin, and I am not indignant? If I

must boast, I will boast of the things that show my weakness. (2 Cor. 11:24–30 NABRE)

Paul was saying that he knew something great was on the other side of suffering, making the suffering worthwhile. Our spiritual sacrifice is for the promise of eternity, and there can be nothing greater. In our temporal world, however, we can compare this sacrifice to going to the gym. We suffer through a workout and the ensuing aches and pains because we know that on the other side of that suffering is fitness, which is ultimately good for us. A pregnant woman endures nine months of discomfort as her body changes to protect the baby growing within, but she knows the other side of that is the miracle of a new life. Students of difficult curricula endure difficult study regimens because the other side of that sacrifice is a professional license.

Paul puts into perspective for us the eternal glory that will make our earthly sacrifices pale in comparison. A million years in eternity will diminish the sacrifices we experience in this world to no more than a grain of sand on a vast beach.

The Scripture passage that resonates even more with my decision to enter into and remain in ministry is this: "But rejoice to the extent that you share in the sufferings of Christ, so that when his glory is revealed you may also rejoice exultantly" (1 Pet. 4:13 NABRE). There's joy in participating in Christ's suffering.

Think about the saying "Misery loves company." We often consider this a negative sentiment, that the miserable want others to be miserable, too, but there's another way to look at this. It is easier to bear our burdens when others share the load. Again, let's look at the temporal examples. It's easier to endure a rigorous physical workout with a gym partner. It's easier to prepare for a major exam when we have a study partner. It's easier to go into space with a team of astronauts. It's easier to fight a war with a platoon. It's easier to get through difficult times when we have company.

Now, think about sharing in Christ's suffering, Christ is our partner with us in every difficult moment. As St. Catherine of Siena once said, "Nothing great is ever achieved without much enduring."

As in any calling, it is important that we ministers count our blessings. I love seeing someone being transformed and drawn closer to Jesus Christ. There is no greater feeling for me as a minister knowing that the gospel I preach caused someone's life to be transformed, leaving the way of the world and accepting the way of our Lord Jesus. Whenever we experience such high-level moments in life, those blessings, we should make note of them. Count those blessings. Name them one by one. Write them in a journal, make a mental note, or keep a box of index cards, each with a blessing or a nice remark or compliment we received. Practice gratitude. When someone pays us a compliment, we should thank them but also document their remark, if it indeed moved us. Then, in times of doubt, when we feel down, we need to take that box out and read those compliments, blessings, and thank-you notes. Remember to never get too high on the highs or too low on the lows. We know there will be ups and downs in this life. It's all part of the challenge and sacrifice in preparation for eternal life with God.

Let's walk in faith. Let's take faith outside of just the mind and the heart and let faith be in our deeds and our actions. May we show our faith to the whole world. When others see us, may they know by how we live, even more than how we speak, that we are people of faith.

Reflection Questions

- Think of an instance in your life that shook your faith. What questions did you have, and how were they answered? Did you seek counsel, spend more time in prayer, or fall out of faith for a time?

- Fear is a powerful emotion. It can weaken us if we let it. Unfortunately, we often succumb to the crippling effects of fear and worry, yet we know faith and fear cannot live together. In addition to prayer, what habits can you form to increase your faith in God and God's plan for your life?

- Consider a time when you encouraged others to keep the faith. What words of wisdom did you offer?

- Consider a time when you faced a dire situation yet remained calm and faithful. What was the outcome of that situation? Do you reflect upon that experience when you find yourself becoming fearful? Have you shared that example to bring faith to others?

Note

[1] Smokey Robinson & The Miracles, "The Tears of a Clown," written by Hank Cosby, Smokey Robinson, and Stevie Wonder, track 6 on side 2 on *Make It Happen*, Hitsville USA, 1967.

6

TRANSFORMATION

In the pursuit of a harmonious and fulfilling life, we often find ourselves entangled in the relentless pursuit of productivity and success, forgetting the fundamental need for rest and rejuvenation. In a society where busyness is applauded and laziness frowned upon, we sometimes overlook the significance of finding a balance between work and rest. Yet, within the pages of the Bible, we discover a timeless principle that speaks directly to this essential aspect of our lives—the Sabbath rest principle. Rooted in the scriptural passage of Hebrews 4:1–11, this principle illuminates the transformation from rigid legalism in Sabbath keeping to a more profound understanding of the underlying principle: the call to rest. While the observance of a specific day may have changed, the essence of rest remains unchanged. This chapter delves into the biblical narrative, reveals God's intention behind the Sabbath, and challenges us to embrace the restful principle that extends far beyond a single day. As followers of Christ, we are beckoned to seek rest not only for our bodies but also for our souls, recognizing it as an act of obedience, an affirmation of God's grace, and a celebration of his creation and redemption. Embracing this principle will undoubtedly require effort and sacrifice, but the reward is immeasurable—a deeper connection with God and a more fulfilling and balanced life.

We take many things for granted, including simple things like toilets and running water, electricity, and paved roads. We can become so busy that we forget how important it is to drink water or to have access to clean water, which gives and sustains life on this planet. In our society, being immersed in busyness, overactivity, and chaos is often seen as noble, a cause for pride or something to be praised and admired. I challenge anyone to find a single verse in the Bible where being extraordinarily busy is celebrated.

Conversely, we know it is sinful to be lazy. We know it's wrong to be a sloth, and we don't like lazy folks. In fact, we dislike laziness so much that we sometimes assume the reason anyone falls into misfortune is laziness. We admire hard work. We love hard workers. We hate and despise laziness.

As God's children and as followers of Jesus, we are called to a different worldview. I believe we are called to understand and observe the Sabbath rest principle. People often ask me, "Do we practice the Sabbath or not? What day is the Sabbath?" I usually start my answer by explaining that the Sabbath is on Saturday. The Sabbath day never changed to Sunday. It is Saturday. It has always been Saturday and will forever be Saturday. Furthermore, we are still supposed to practice the Sabbath. We know that rest is important to God. In Genesis 1, we see how God created our world, our universe, and all that is in it. Chapter 2 of Genesis begins, "Thus the heavens and the earth were finished, and all their multitude. And . . . [God] rested on the seventh day from all the work that he had done" (Gen. 2:1–2).

God rested. He completed his task and took time to rest and relax. As we see in Exodus 20:8–11, God commands that we rest on the Sabbath day. Stay with me here. Not just the Hebrew people or those who practice the Hebrew religion, but also the animals and the alien residents. This Sabbath was an act of grace. It set apart the Hebrew people from other ancient Near Eastern lands and countries and societies where people would work the slaves and the animals to death and where they themselves did not take time to rest.

It is sinful to work so much that we never find time to assemble with the people of God, let alone take time to rest. Rest is commanded in the Bible. God takes rest so seriously that in the law, as we'll see later, man was to provide a day of rest for slaves and animals, too. We often focus on several scriptures anchored in Hebrews 4, the entire chapter, but if we need a place to lay our hats, we can lay them on verses 8–11:

> For if Joshua had given them rest, God would not speak later about another day. So then, a sabbath rest still remains for the people of God; for those who enter God's rest also cease from their labors as God did from his. Let us therefore make every effort to enter that rest, so that no one may fall through such disobedience as theirs.

The word *sabbath* in Hebrew means to cease, desist. It means to stop work or to rest. Some commentators give different reasons for why God issued a Sabbath on the seventh day, but I believe God understands the benefit and importance of taking a moment to rest, to celebrate God's creation.

Now, I know that some have a hard time imagining a God so graceful. Unfortunately, many people see God only as a stern taskmaster in the heavens. Instead, we should see God as a graceful parent, leading us and directing us to the divine.

The Sabbath day is Saturday because, in the creation accounts, we see that God rested on the seventh day. It is an integral part of the creation. It was codified in the Ten Commandments. The seventh day of the seven-day week cycle (that day is Saturday) is the day God rested. Now, there are examples of the early church gathering on the first day of the week, which is Sunday, but there are also examples of the early church meeting to teach and to worship on the Sabbath day. For reference, read Acts 13:14, 27, and 42–44. Also, study Acts 15:21, 16:13, 17:2, and 18:4, 20. Acts 13:42–44 is especially significant, because we see Paul and Barnabas were speaking in a Jewish synagogue and were invited to return to speak again the following Sabbath.

God rested on the seventh day of creation, and this is a clear mandate for the necessity of rest! Furthermore, there are examples in the New Testament of the writers participating in some aspects and functions of the Sabbath. As stated before, the word *sabbath* in Hebrew means to rest, to cease. The Sabbath day is a rest day. According to Old Testament law, there were severe penalties for not observing the rest day. For instance, in Exodus 31:14, Scripture says one could be put to death for not obeying the Sabbath. Although it remains uncertain whether the penalty was ever strictly enforced, owing to a scarcity of preserved documentation on the subject, nonetheless, it is known that death was the legal penalty for breaking the Sabbath.

God says, "You shall not do any work—you, or your son or your daughter, or your male or female slave, or your ox or your donkey, or any of your livestock, or the resident alien in your towns, so that your male and female slave may rest as well as you" (Deut. 5:14). We have a five-day workweek because we want to take the weekend to rest. It comes out of the Hebrew religion. It comes out of the faith system: to take a rest.

As the Hebrews participated in the Sabbath, we see that the day began to be a day to meditate and praise God, a day to celebrate the creation. We see an example of this in Isaiah 66:23, where the writer says, "From sabbath to sabbath, all flesh shall come to worship before me, says the LORD." Also, in the New Testament, we see many examples of Jesus and his followers going to synagogues and teaching on the Sabbath: Mark 1:2 and 6:2, Luke 4:16 and 6:6, and Acts 18:4.

I want to stress that the primary function of the Sabbath is to rest and to celebrate God's creation and God's redemption. The Sabbath was a time to meditate on the Lord and to praise God. It's important for us to understand that rooted in the creation of the world itself is rest. Nothing we do can become as fantastic and marvelous and wonderful as the creation itself, but even in the creation by an all-powerful God, the seventh day was reserved for rest. God also wants us to rest.

The beginning of Hebrews 4 instructs, "Therefore, while the promise of entering his rest is still open, let us take care that none of you should seem to have failed to reach it" (Heb. 4:1). The writer is drawing a metaphor. He's using an illustration with the Hebrew people wandering in the desert who were restless and wanted to rest but were not going to find rest until they were in the promised land.

The writer talks about entering into this rest. The *Faithlife Study Bible* notes that for the wilderness generation, "Entry to this rest was more than just a theological metaphor. It represented an end to the wandering that characterized their lives after the exodus, finding peace. Once God's people had already entered into Canaan, the promise of rest still remained. See Psalm 95:7–11."

Many of us, like the Hebrews, are wandering through the desert today because of disobedience. Many are unable to find rest because of disobedience. They are restless. This disobedience can be as simple as not following the command to rest, or it can be as complicated as following our own will and way and finding that is very problematic for living a healthy life, as it results in restlessness. The Hebrews writer is saying that, because of disobedience, the Hebrews weren't able to find rest. This is the metaphor that is strung throughout Hebrews 4:1–11. The writer alludes to Joshua and Caleb's effort to bring a message, just like we have a good message.

> For indeed the good news came to us just as to them; but the message they heard did not benefit them, because they were not united by faith with those who listened. For we who have believed enter that rest, just as God has said, "As in my anger I swore, 'They shall not enter my rest,'" though his works were finished at the foundation of the world. (Heb. 4:2–3)

The writer goes on to explain that those who are disobedient cannot enter Sabbath rest, but for those who are obedient, the rest still remains. Later, in Hebrews 4:8–11, we are taught that we should make every effort to enter into Sabbath rest. If we truly want to enter into *Shabbat* (the Hebrew word for *Sabbath*, which means to cease or to rest), we must be obedient. Simply spending time in rest is being obedient. To ignore or disobey the Sabbath is not resting. To follow God's will is to find rest and to find comfort, knowing you are doing what pleases God.

The Sabbath rest is a both/and situation. Some argue that Sabbath rest is heaven, while others say the Sabbath rest is now. It's both/and. Right now, we have a Sabbath rest that we enter into so we can practice the Sabbath rest principle that is written into creation, but the eternal Sabbath rest comes in the sweet by and by, in heaven, and the eternal fellowship and communion with God.

Make no mistake about it—in this life, we must make every effort to enter into Sabbath rest, and doing so might be a struggle. It might require a serious conversation with an employer. It might require persuading our family to form new habits. It might require rearranging our calendars to ensure we honor Sabbath rest. We know it is both/and because of Hebrews 4:9–10: "So then, a sabbath rest still remains for the people of God; for those who enter God's rest also cease from their labors as God did from his." With conviction, therefore, I repeat, "Remember the Sabbath and keep it holy" (Exod. 20:8 NCB).

We must find time to rest. In the new covenant, it doesn't have to be Saturday, but it must be a time available for you to rest and also find time to meditate on God and to celebrate creation. Rest is important because, truthfully, being a workaholic is a form of idolatry. It is prioritizing work over God. It is prioritizing money over creation. A lot of problems persist in our world because money and greed are prioritized over creation itself.

I did an internship at Sinai Hospital in Baltimore, during which time I encouraged people and worked with the sick. There was a special elevator that did not require pressing buttons to operate it. It stopped at each floor. It reminds me of the Sabbath. Those who observe the Sabbath can get in that elevator without having to hit a button, without having to labor. This is the way the Sabbath is observed and fought for.

Are we prepared to advocate for our Sabbath rest as well? Are we ready to stand up for our moments of reflection, meditation, and simple rest? Consider how adherents of various faith traditions, including Islam, value and prioritize their prayer times, often making concerted efforts to integrate these practices into their daily lives. This dedication to spiritual observance can inspire us in our own commitment to Sabbath rest.

Are we willing to fight to make sure that at least we have time to assemble with the saints on Sunday? Are we willing to fight just to make sure we have time to rest so we won't have to fall into the idolatry of workaholism? If we work without resting, we risk not making time for God, and we all know who snakes his way into that void. Why aren't many Christians willing to fight for our Sabbath rest? We must make room for it. To do so is to resist the idolatry of this age.

Guided by Prayer

I sometimes have long, drawn-out thoughts about my landline. *Is it really worth it?* Because of all the telemarketing calls, I wonder if I want to keep it. While minding my business recently, I received a call from a company I had never heard of. The caller asked me to participate in a survey. This company wanted my ideas and my thoughts, but I'd never heard of the company, and I just couldn't get over the fact that I didn't know how they were going to use the data. I tried to google the company, and I couldn't find any information about them, so I told them, "Unfortunately, I will not be taking your survey today," and they immediately hung up on me.

Shortly after that incident, I discovered that all my travel points had disappeared. I had been saving these travel points for years. I didn't know what I was going to use them on, but all the travel points were zeroed out. I was not happy about it, so I called the airline. I called the corporate office, and I spoke with a representative who helped me get my points back. For the past several years, I, forgetfully, did not register some of my flights with my number, and because of that, they erased my points. Thankfully, the airline rep, who was kind to me, helped me get all my points back. The rep asked me, "At the end of this call, would you take a survey?" I said, "Yes. Absolutely, I want to take your survey." It's interesting whom we want to talk to and whom we don't want to talk to. The fact is, I felt more comfortable talking to the airline rep than the random telemarketer because the airline rep and I had become familiar with each other.

The contrast of the two incidents made me think about prayer. How come God gets so little time? Is it because, like the telemarketer, we don't think we know God well enough? Is that why? Or is it because we aren't familiar enough with God? Is there a connection between our prayer lives and our closeness to God? God wants to hear from us. He created us to have a relationship with him, so why do we at times resist talking to God? We must not treat God like a telemarketer, avoiding conversations with him at all costs.

Let's shift focus to a discussion about celebrity status. When we encounter someone famous, we immediately want to commemorate the occasion. In the past, that usually meant requesting an autograph. I remember hearing stories about some celebrities becoming so tired of being asked for autographs that they would wear a cast on their arm just so people would avoid requesting a signature. These days, there's no escape. Fans say, "It's fine. I don't mind if you have a cast on your arm. Let's take a selfie." Anyone who has spent any time on the Internet is familiar with the selfie, a photo someone takes of himself or herself. Some people are quite good at stretching out their arm with the phone positioned just so and capturing a photo of themselves, alone or with another person or a group of people. Interestingly, the selfie in many ways has replaced the autograph.

Think about this. When people meet celebrities—actors, singers, athletes, politicians, writers—they get so excited. They get up close and personal with people who seem larger than life, who are rich and "cool," who are adored by millions. Now let's put that excitement into context. As Christians, followers of Jesus, we have a direct connection to the maker and creator of the universe. We have an immediate line to the alpha and the omega, the beginning and the end, the eternal God. That's a connection that should get us excited. God wants to hear from all of us. Praying to God is a privilege, and every saint is required to have a prayer life.

Remember the three P's of prayer life: practice, persistence, and patience. Begin with 1 Thessalonians 5:17, "Pray without ceasing." We are to pray to God all the time. We are to tell God about our dreams, our fears, our anger. Some of us have problems developing the kind of relationship with God that we want because we approach God as a drill sergeant or a school principal. We approach God timidly and say, "Excuse me, sir. God, sir, is it okay if I ask you a couple of things, if I could just give you a couple of petitions? You know what, God? I bet you're too busy. I'll just come back another day."

Hebrews 4:16 says we can approach the throne of grace boldly. God is our parent, our Abba. We don't have to approach God as though we are approaching some tyrant or dictator, trembling in fear. No, we should approach God like God is, which is our parent. The word *Abba*, which means "Father," is a term of endearment like "Daddy" or "Mommy," an intimate name between a child and a parent.

Parents, imagine how it would feel if your children always approached you as if they were full of fear, scared to say anything to you at all. I mean, just full of absolute fear. Would you feel that they understood how much you loved them? If they approached you like this all the time, would you wonder, "Do these children really know how much I love them? How have I treated my children to make them want to approach me so timidly and so afraid to have an intimate conversation with me, so afraid to tell me about what's really going on in their lives?"

God is our parent, and we can approach God with how we really feel. It's unfortunate that prayer can become so ritualistic that we forget God is a person we are talking to. God is not a woman or a man; God is a spirit, but God's spirit has personhood. God is a person. You are talking to a person who is the creator of everything we see, feel, hear, taste, and know, and this person is not a person we should ignore or avoid.

We are so grateful for the blood of Christ, as taught in Hebrews 12, because it has made us clean in preparation to approach God's throne. When we approach God's throne timidly or are afraid to be frank, open, and honest with God, we are saying something about the blood of Christ. We are saying the blood of Christ is impotent, that it's not strong enough for us to approach God's throne of grace boldly.

We must be truthful with God. We must be honest with God. We must tell God exactly how we feel. If I am angry, I must tell God I am angry even if I'm angry with God. Doesn't God already know? Of course, God knows. When I have doubts, it may be because of something going on in my life, and it may cause me to struggle with my faith. I must bring those doubts to God.

The last person I should bring those doubts to is a worldly person who is far away from God. The best person to bring my doubts to is God. God is big enough to handle our honesty.

When we begin to understand that God truly wants to hear from us, we must be persistent. In Luke 11:5–8, Jesus demonstrates just how committed to prayer we are to be as he says,

> Suppose one of you has a friend, and you go to him at midnight and say to him, "Friend, lend me three loaves of bread; for a friend of mine has arrived, and I have nothing to set before him." And he answers from within, "Do not bother me; the door has already been locked, and my children are with me in bed; I cannot get up and give you anything." I tell you, even though he will not get up and give him anything because he is his friend, at least because of his persistence he will get up and give him whatever he needs.

Like this neighbor, sometimes we feel that God is too big for our small problems, but instead, Jesus uses this illustration about a neighbor who didn't have enough food to feed his guest to talk about why we should be persistent in our prayer. We must get real about persistently letting God know about the petitions of our hearts, like this neighbor who continued to knock and persisted until his neighbor opened the door.

This is the way we must pray to God. Continue. Persist. Continue to ask. Continue to knock. This is what Jesus is trying to say. This neighbor wasn't quick to jump up and open the door, yet Jesus says to keep knocking. When we feel that God has not answered our prayers, we are to continue to knock. Even when we feel that our problems are too small for a big God to care about, we are to continue praying. Nothing is too small for God. If God has the hairs on our heads numbered, imagine how God feels about our concerns, about our petitions, about our worries. God is not too big or busy for any of our problems. Our God cares.

In my ministry, I experience a lot of people who talk about their prayer life. Some have told me that they do not think God has time for their little issues. I've been told by some that they do not feel they should bring their issues to God because, although their issues are big to them, they are too small for God. This is human projection. *Encyclopedia Britannica* defines *projection* as "the mental process by which people attribute to others what is in their own minds."[1] When we feel that God cannot be bothered with our small problems, we are projecting onto God how we might react if we were all-powerful and all-knowing.

I recall a time when President Obama was filmed walking through the White House on his way to a meeting and encountered a janitor and fist-bumped him. The man who held the highest office in the country and the world turned his attention to an ordinary worker and elevated that person, if only in that instance. Not everyone is like that. Some would not make time for those who they felt were beneath them. I imagine those who do make time for anyone might have an easier time recognizing that God can also make time for anyone.

God is not like us. God has every hair on our heads numbered, just as Matthew 10:29–31 says. God has his eye on a sparrow, a small bird, so we know God is watching us. God cares about each of us on a personal level and on a collective level. God cares so much that he sent his only begotten Son to die on a cross for us, so that we would have life. It is important for us to remember that we can and should go to God all the time in prayer. God is not like us. He will not look down on us, he is not too busy for us, and he will not turn us away. God will walk with us through the challenges we face in life.

Now that we have established that God expects our persistence, we must come to terms with waiting on his response. This period of waiting requires patience. In Psalm 27:14, we are told, "Wait for the Lord; be strong, and let your heart take courage; wait for the Lord!" I'll be honest—waiting on the Lord is hard for a lot of us to do. It's hard because we struggle with when and where and how we should wait. We struggle with the balance of action and patience.

I suggest that we constantly work progressively toward God's purpose for us. When we reach roadblocks or when we have a hard time finding a key to a lock, we need to wait on the Lord, but while we wait, we should still try to, in a righteous way, deconstruct the roadblock and open the door. The problem with waiting on the Lord is that some people resort to using sin to open the door. We try to insist on our own carnal ways to get past the impending roadblock. We get in trouble when we use sin instead of patience. Waiting on the Lord doesn't mean I stop doing what God has planned for me. It means I continue to work while I wait for God to help me get over the hurdle.

What if I say, "I want to have a flower garden," but I have problems finding seeds for my flower garden? I can continue to till the ground. I can continue to prepare the soil. I can continue to get ready for the seeds while waiting for them. That's working through the roadblock. I could say, "I don't want to wait on the Lord," but what would I gain? The principle behind this simple analogy can be applied to complex ethical issues.

Waiting on the Lord is not an absence of good works. To wait on the Lord is to wait for God to provide a righteous way to fulfill what we believe is God's purpose for us.

In Luke 18, Jesus tells a parable about a persistent widow and a judge who wasn't righteous. The persistent widow had something done to her that wasn't right. She went to the judge to get justice. The judge did not give it to her. She got up and continued to knock on the judge's door until the Lord softened the judge's heart, and she found her justice. In her case, not waiting on the Lord could have resulted in her possibly murdering the judge or resorting to something sinful to get what she wanted. Instead, she persisted while she prayed that God would open the door that had been locked. She did not resort to sin.

Waiting on the Lord is not giving up. It's not a lazy endeavor where we sit back and watch and wait. Waiting on the Lord is continuing to use our hands and feet and mind while waiting for the Lord to push us closer to his plan for us. "But seek first the kingdom of God and his righteousness, and all these things will be given you besides" (Matt. 6:33 NABRE).

Let us not look at prayer as a chore. Prayer is not doing God a favor. Prayer is not a waste of time. It is not futile to pray. It's not a waste of your breath. Prayer isn't always reciting words. Prayer is a conversation with God. It's a privilege and a joy, and we should treat it as such.

Reflection Questions

▶ Do you consider working six or seven days a week noble or sinful? Why?

▶ What is your immediate reaction to the idea of observing the Sabbath, reserving one day each week to rest?

▶ Failing to make time for rest, reflection, and prayer is sinful. Laziness is also sinful, but have you ever considered busyness to be a sign of laziness? According to Tim Ferriss, author of *The 4-Hour Work Week*, "Being busy is a form of laziness—lazy thinking and indiscriminate action."[2] What is your reaction to this concept?

▶ Businessman LeRoy Carlson famously said, "What you do on Saturdays is what puts you ahead of the competition." On the surface, it sounds like Carlson was implying that working when others were playing may provide competitive advantage, but I submit that a day allocated to rest and reflection with God is the key to success. Understanding God's intention for a Sabbath day of rest, how will you structure your week from this point forward?

▶ Identify three ways to increase your prayer life. Which of these methods can you begin putting into practice this week?

▶ When you feel your prayers are not being answered, do you give up, adjust your approach, or pray for understanding? How often do you pray "Your will be done" (Matt. 6:10)?

Notes

[1] Nancy McWilliams, *Encyclopedia Britannica Online*, s.v. "projection," February 29, 2024, https://www.britannica.com/science/projection-psychology.

[2] Tim Ferriss, "'Productivity' Tricks for the Neurotic, Manic-Depressive, and Crazy (Like Me)," *Tim Ferriss* (blog), November 3, 2013, https://tim.blog/2013/11/03/productivity-hacks/.

7

FORGIVENESS

Saint Augustine of Hippo said, "The confession of evil works is the beginning of good works."[1] Think back to elementary school. Nobody liked the kid who always snitched. "Oh, you're a tell. You're just a tattletale." We all knew somebody who was like, "I'm going to tell," the second things got a little dicey. He could not wait to tell the teacher everything his classmates did. Nobody liked that person. Even some teachers didn't like the tattletales.

In our Christian walk, we must develop the habit and practice of telling on ourselves, confessing our sinfulness and our need for redemption, and accepting the reality that each of us is flawed. We must understand that we will make mistakes and that we are saved by the blood of the Lamb. I believe confession is a healing balm. Everyone needs healing. We all need growth. We can neither heal nor grow without confession. We must confess.

"For all have sinned and come short of the glory of God" (Rom. 3:23 KJ21). We all have sins to confess. First John 1:9 says,

"If we confess our sins, he who is faithful and just will forgive us our sins and cleanse us from all unrighteousness." Our ability to confess our sins is the first step to being forgiven. Also, we cannot heal if we refuse to confess our sins. James 5:16 makes this plain, reminding us, "Therefore confess your sins to one another, and pray for one another, so that you may be healed. The prayer of the righteous is powerful and effective."

Why should we confess? Because God commanded us to do so. James 5:16 makes it clear. It requires humility to confess our faults. The opposite of humility is pridefulness. Excessive pride is sinful; it's how we become monsters. When we refuse or simply forget to confess our sins, we fool ourselves into thinking we are perfect. This is why prayer, meditation, and reflection are so vital to our spiritual growth. God promises us mercy. Proverbs 28:13 says, "No one who conceals transgressions will prosper, but one who confesses and forsakes them will obtain mercy."

While some have disconnected from confession because they are too prideful and arrogant to admit when they are wrong, for others it is a matter of fear of the consequences. The offense is already there, and God already knows what we've done, so there's no need to be afraid. It reminds me of a child who sneaks a cookie out of the cookie jar. The conversation begins:

"Did you take the cookie?"

"No."

"Just tell me. Did you take the cookie?"

The child repeats, "No."

"I just want to make sure I'm not going crazy. I know there were six cookies. Now there are five. Did *you take the cookie? If you tell me the truth, I will not punish you."*

Then the child reluctantly says, "Okay. I took the cookie."

"Okay. Do not do it anymore."

The Bible says God will show mercy if we confess. So why pretend we are perfect or have not transgressed?

In confession, we find mercy. Confession has benefits. Confession protects community. This is why James 5:16 says: "Confess one to another" (AMPC). Confession will protect our community. "Therefore confess your sins to one another, and pray for one another, so that you may be healed. The prayer of the righteous is powerful and effective." Where there is no confession, there can be no community.

Lack of confession breeds hypocrisy. We have all heard people say, "I don't go to church because the church is full of hypocrites." People who say this are not necessarily saying they have a problem with churchgoers because we have sinned. Instead, they have a problem with churchgoers who refuse to admit to having sinned. We turn off members of the community when we refuse to admit that we are wrapped up in the same human condition as everyone else and put on airs of perfection.

Despite all the fronting, God still sees our every imperfection. The word *hypocrite* in Greek simply means "actor." If the community were a confessing community, no one would call us hypocrites because we would recognize that we are flawed, that we are sinners, that we are broken, that we aren't perfect, and that we need Jesus.

In a confessing community, people don't hold grudges, because instead of holding grudges against one another, we are praying for one another. I heard somebody say once that it's impossible to hold a grudge against someone you are praying for. "Therefore confess your sins to one another, and pray for one another, so that you may be healed. The prayer of the righteous is powerful and effective" (James 5:16).

What shall we confess? We must confess our faults, our sins, our pride, and our unbelief. Proverbs 29:23 says, "A person's pride will bring humiliation, but one who is lowly in spirit will obtain honor." Whatever the Holy Spirit reveals to us we should confess. The Holy Spirit will help us see what we cannot see in ourselves.

Writing about her time as a field agent with the Central Intelligence Agency, Amaryllis Fox shared on Facebook, "If I learned one lesson from my time with the CIA, it is this: everybody believes they are the good guy."

Hollywood has us fooled into thinking there's an evil person who knows they are evil and is intentionally out there doing evil. That's not reality. Not all who commit evil deeds are dastardly villains like the Riddler or the Joker. Most people think they are doing what is right. They think they are doing what is good. *The road to hell is paved with good intentions.* Most people do not know they are behaving in an evil way. If we don't listen to the Holy Spirit, we will never know.

The Holy Spirit will sometimes even use our enemies to communicate truths to us. Amaryllis Fox said we need to listen to our enemies to learn another perspective about ourselves. Brothers and sisters, we need the Holy Spirit's conviction to show us when we are wrong. We need the Holy Spirit's conviction to show us when we have transgressed.

If we are disconnected from the Holy Spirit, we will always think we are right, and we will never realize we are wrong. We will go through life hardly ever apologizing, never repenting, and never reconciling. People disconnected from the Holy Spirit hardly ever repent and confess their faults because the Holy Spirit is not in them to convict them. Instead, pride grows and makes them feel that they are like God and without sin. Some of us need to invite the Holy Spirit into our hearts so that the Holy Spirit can reveal to us our sins and lead us to confess and repent.

To whom shall we confess? We confess to God our Father. "If we confess our sins, he who is faithful and just will forgive us our sins and cleanse us from all unrighteousness" (1 John 1:9). To whom shall we confess? To those against whom we have sinned. "So when you are offering your gift at the altar . . ." (Matt. 5:23–24). We are offering a gift at the altar. We may have offered a financial gift, but we are also offering the gift of time to God. Matthew continues, ". . . if you remember that your brother or sister has something against you, leave your gift there before the altar and go; first be reconciled to your brother or sister, and then come and offer your gift." These are the words of Jesus. Jesus doesn't want our worship if we can't reconcile with our brother or sister.

To whom shall we confess? To those whose faith in Jesus has been hindered by us. How has my behavior affected somebody else, keeping him or her from following Jesus? Has my behavior brought people closer to Jesus or pushed people farther away from Jesus? I confess to them that I'm sorry I have not been the example they needed, but I can do better. To whom shall we confess? To one another. Remember James 5:16: "Therefore confess your sins to one another, and pray for one another, so that you may be healed. The prayer of the righteous is powerful and effective."

What will happen when we confess? We will receive forgiveness. From 1 John 1:9, again: "If we confess our sins, he who is faithful and just will forgive us our sins and cleanse us from all unrighteousness. If we say that we have not sinned, we make him a liar, and his word is not in us."

What will happen if we confess? Our prayers will become effective. Hear me now. Some people, even those who pray fervently and frequently, wonder why their prayers don't seem very effective. It's because of their lack of confession. If we confess our sins, God is faithful and just and will forgive us and cleanse us from all unrighteousness.

If we confess our sins, we will be healed. Scripture tells us, "Therefore confess your sins to one another, and pray for one another, so that you may be healed. The prayer of the righteous is powerful and effective." Our prayers are weak and puny because we have not accepted a confessional spirit. If we want powerful and effective prayers, we must confess. We must approach the throne of God with humility and understand that we are only there because we are saved by the blood of the Lamb.

We all approach the altar with sin, with faults. We have hurt others, and we feel as though we cannot be healed. We feel as though we can get no relief. We feel guilty. We feel dirty, all because of our refusal to confess.

When we confess our wrongs, we are cleansed and purified. When we confess, our vision becomes clear, and we can better understand God's righteousness. When we confess, we hear God's appointments for service in Jesus's name. I believe it's time for every one of us to have a personal revival. It's time to confess. I'm not talking about confessing somebody else's sin. It's time to tattle on ourselves. As sung in the old hymn, "It's me, it's me, it's me, O Lord, standing in the need of prayer."

I Need Forgiveness

I try to do right by people. I try to treat others as I want to be treated. I know, however, that no matter how hard we try, we will all offend someone one day. Each of us plays the offender from time to time, and each of us needs to seek forgiveness.

When seeking forgiveness, remember these four "I" statements:

- I am sorry.
- I repent.
- I need forgiveness.
- I will make restitution.

Let's examine the phrase "I am sorry." Apologizing is akin to saying, "I am sorrowful." *I am full of sorrow for what I have done.* Apologizing requires courage—courage to admit having done wrong. A lot of people lack the courage or humility to make an apology. Some will immediately resort to pointing the finger at another, playing the blame game to take the onus off themselves. Some might try playing the tit-for-tat game: "Well, remember the time you . . . ," simply to avoid apologizing.

Saying "I am sorry" does not have the same direction as "I repent," because we can fall into the habit of saying "I am sorry" and then repeating the offense over and over. There is another way to apologize, which is to say, "I repent." The difference between saying "I am sorry" and "I repent" is that the latter contains an imperative to change. When I say, "I am sorry," I am not making a commitment to change unless my sorrow is coupled with repenting. Repenting has direction. It means that I have made a conscious decision to make a change. *I will change my behavior. I will no longer harm you.*

The word *repent* in Greek means to change one's mind and to feel remorse. To repent means I am both sorrowful and remorseful and that I am going to change my behavior.

When we repent to God, we must begin with the person we see in the mirror. Luke 13 begins with the crowd telling Jesus about the Galileans whose blood Pilate had mingled with their sacrifices. Jesus responded with the point that the crowd needn't worry about the Galileans but about themselves. He told them to repent lest they perish as the Galileans did or as the eighteen who were killed when the tower of Siloam fell upon them. Essentially, he was telling the crowd not to judge others but to be concerned about their own judgment day.

Jesus tells us that we have to keep a watchful eye on ourselves, on our own transgressions. When we repent, it means we have decided to follow Jesus. It means we are no longer trying to do things our way, to build our own empire or our own kingdom, but that we are trying to follow Jesus. When we repent to God, we are saying, *Thank you, Lord, for this gift of free will. I accept it and am choosing to do your will, not mine. I want to follow you, God. I do not want to be led by my own carnal desires. I repent for my arrogance, my lack of humility, my lack of prayer, my failure to follow you. Now I am going to follow you as I should have all along. I realize that if I do not follow you, God, I will perish.*

Once we repent to God, we then must repent to one another. It is not a one-way street. Replying to one of the scribes, who asked which was the greatest of all the commandments, Jesus said to love God entirely—heart, soul, and strength—in essence, to give our entire being to God. He then said that the second is to love our neighbors as ourselves. "There is no other commandment greater than these" (Mark 12:31). God is not interested in a love that leaves out God's children. If you love God, you must also love God's children. Imagine a visitor coming to our home who loves us but hates our children. Do we want that person staying in our home? If the visitor poses any threat to our children, we are going to escort him out of our home.

We have to mind how we treat one another. In Luke 17, Jesus instructs us to mind our actions, saying if someone sins against us and repents, we must forgive them. Even if they sin against us seven times and repent seven times, we are to forgive them each time. When someone repents to us, he is also repenting to God; therefore, we must forgive as God would. It may not be easy, especially when a person sins against us seven times. If that person repents seven times, we must forgive. It will not be fun. It will not feed our flesh. It will not satisfy our flesh or quell our anger, but it follows Jesus.

Keep in mind that forgiveness is not devoid of accountability. Jesus said to rebuke to hold the sinner accountable. Then he said that the repentant sinner is demonstrating accountability, a willingness to change. After that genuine repentance, we are under obligation to forgive. Our relationship with one another has a direct impact on our relationship with God.

> We love because he first loved us. Whoever claims to love God yet hates a brother or sister is a liar; for whoever does not love their brother and sister, whom they have seen, cannot love God, whom they have not seen. And he has given us this command: Anyone who loves God must also love their brother and sister. (1 John 4:19–21 NIV)

These are tough words to digest, but these are the words of God. It is worth repeating: our relationship with one another has a direct impact on our relationship with God. We cannot love God but hate God's children. We must love one another. If we offend each other, we must repent to one another. Jesus even says that he doesn't want our gift at the altar or worship until we work out our differences.

We know people in our lives who are rough and need forgiveness, but we also know that none of us is without blemish. We all need forgiveness from God. We all need to ask each other forgiveness from time to time because we "all have sinned and fall short of the glory of God" (Rom. 3:23). As Christians, we must get used to the posture of forgiveness. We will all need to forgive. Likewise, we will all need to repent for ways we offend each other.

"I Need Forgiveness" is the title of this section and the third "I" statement we need to make a regular part of our lexicon. I know that I am a flawed man. I am not perfect. I make mistakes. I know that it is only by the grace of God that I go. Therefore, I am quick to forgive because I want God to forgive me. Jesus said, "For if you forgive others their trespasses, your heavenly Father will also forgive you; but if you do not forgive others, neither will your Father forgive your trespasses" (Matt. 6:14–15).

I want God to forgive me. I know I need it. For that reason, I forgive others like I want God to forgive me. We must forgive one another as we want God to forgive us. We must remember the importance of repentance, as Jesus said in Luke 17:3—if we want to be forgiven by someone, we must repent from the offense we committed. God wants us to repent for our sins against him and against one another. After our repentance, God forgives freely, and we must do the same. Forgiveness is powerful and likely one of the most challenging disciplines mentioned in this book. Every day, we need to forgive someone—maybe someone who cut us off in traffic, who was rude to us at the grocery store, who lied about us on the job, or who hindered us from getting what we think we deserve. But imagine carrying around all the bitterness and anger for a lack of forgiveness forever. Imagine being poisoned but refusing the antidote because you don't want to let the poisoner off the hook. That's what not forgiving looks like. Holding grudges damages important relationships for years, if not indefinitely.

We cannot reasonably expect the injured to forgive without also expecting the injurer to ameliorate the harm they have caused. This concept is reflected in the interconnection between the fourth and third statements, highlighting that forgiveness from the injured and restitution by the injurer are mutually dependent. This principle is illustrated in the story of Zacchaeus, who, upon being confronted by Jesus for his actions as an exploitative tax collector, did more than merely express regret and seek forgiveness; he also repaid fourfold what he had stolen, as documented in Luke 19:8. It constitutes an injustice in itself to ask for forgiveness from the injured while they continue to endure the consequences of the injury, without demanding that the injurer provide restitution and fully contribute to restoring their well-being. True forgiveness becomes a collective obligation only when it is accompanied by sincere repentance and appropriate restitution.

Despite how difficult forgiveness or any discipline in this book can be, we can do it with God, with the strength of the Holy Spirit, the witness of Jesus, and the never-ending love of the Father! That's why we need God every hour, to commit to the life of being transformed in Christ; this is the inward revolution, the sanctifying work.

Reflection Questions

▶ Consider times when you are reluctant to confess your sins. What are the top three things that cause you to be reluctant?

▶ Think of a time when you readily confessed a sin. Describe how that confession made you feel and how you felt about your relationship with God.

▶ Think about a situation where someone sought to confess to you. How did you handle it? How might you handle that situation in the future?

▶ Have you ever struggled to forgive someone, or claimed to forgive them but held a grudge in your heart? What can you do to remedy a situation like that?

▶ If you've ever struggled to forgive yourself, remember that our all-knowing, all-powerful God loves each and every one of us. If God can forgive us, shouldn't we have the ability to forgive ourselves? If we cannot forgive ourselves, are we putting ourselves above our almighty God? What is your reaction to this notion?

Note

[1] See Tractate 12, Chapter 3:6–21, sec. 13 of Augustine's *Homilies on the Gospel of John*, in *Nicene and Post-Nicene Fathers*, series 1, vol. 7, ed. Philip Schaff (Grand Rapids: Eerdmans, 1888), 136, available through the Christian Classics Ethereal Library, www.ccel.org/ccel/schaff/npnf107.html.

PRACTICUM

8

SPIRITUAL DISCIPLINES
A Practical Guide

Scripture says we are presenting our physical bodies at the altar throughout our lives. Too often, many believers fail to remember that when we pray, fast, and sing, we are engaging in both physical and spiritual actions. The physical and spiritual are intertwined—everything we do is intertwined with the spiritual. Therefore, as living, breathing examples of the gospel, we must consciously renew our minds and souls so that we can properly represent. We must practice spiritual disciplines to discern God's will, to know what is good and acceptable.

Spiritual disciplines became important to me when I realized, as a clergyperson, that there are many of us who struggle with depression. According to a 2013 Duke University report, the rate of depression among clergy was slightly over 11 percent, which was double the national average.[1] Anxiety rates were even higher, at 13.5 percent. Not unlike the rest of the nation, those figures skyrocketed between 2020 and 2022, when feelings of isolation and political polarization intensified the stressors clergy already faced. According to a 2023 report from the Barna Group, "pastors' confidence and satisfaction in their vocation has decreased significantly in the past few years, and two in five (41%) say they've considered quitting ministry in the last 12 months."[2] Sadly, a number of clergy succumb to depression, ending their own lives.

The pulpit can be a lonely place. While clergymen and clergywomen are an excellent resource for congregants during times of personal struggle, there are few people with whom they can discuss their own struggles. If a clergyperson is struggling with depression, addiction, or any typical human malady, opening up about it could turn scandalous. The risk of being fired is real.

Clergy are held to a higher standard, understandably, but with that comes the perception of infallibility, which is unrealistic. If a clergyperson says he or she is struggling with depression, there's also the risk that someone will accuse the leader of lacking faith, so the clergyperson bottles up his or her emotions.

Financial struggles are also a major cause of depression. Clergy study the Bible, not finance, in school, so without the support of a finance expert, their bookkeeping can rapidly deteriorate, thus becoming a mess. Some clergy suffer from the weight of family problems, as their children and families are constantly under a microscope, expected to be examples of perfection to the rest of the congregation. As a result of all these pressures, clergy can easily fall into poor devotional habits.

Each of us, ordained clergy and the faithful alike, should be reminded regularly of Jesus's practice of stepping away from the noise to devote time in prayer to God, as outlined in Chapter Two. Practicing spiritual disciplines will help us resist being conformed to this world. Practicing spiritual disciplines will help us promote our own transformation from the temporal to the spiritual.

Much of my research comes from Richard J. Foster's book *Celebration of Discipline*. He defines three modes of resistance: inward disciplines, such as prayer, fasting, meditation, and study; outward disciplines, such as simplicity, solitude, submission, and service; and corporate disciplines, such as confession, worship, guidance, celebration—those things that we do with the community. Read more about this in Chapter Ten.

Other books that have had a tremendous impact on me and that I recommend include: Howard Thurman's *Meditations of the Heart* and *The Inward Journey*, Thomas Keating's *Open Mind, Open Heart*, and Barbara Holmes's *Joy Unspeakable: Contemplative Practices of the Black Church*.

Throughout the Bible are examples of Jesus practicing disciplines. In just a few verses of Matthew 4, Jesus demonstrates several disciplines by going into the desert to pray. He was obedient and submitted to God's will. Jesus went into the desert alone to practice solitude. He prayed, fasted, and meditated. Let's examine what it means to meditate. The purpose of meditation is to free our minds so that we can hear God more clearly. Meditation is listening to, sensing, and heeding the life and light of Christ. This strikes precisely at the heart of our faith. The life that pleases God is not a set of religious duties; it is listening to God's voice and obeying God's Word.

When Jesus encountered the evil one, he practiced simplicity. His "yes" meant "yes" and his "no" meant "no" (Matt. 5:37). Jesus responded to the devil by citing Scripture. How can we incorporate Jesus's example into our own lives? Spiritual disciplines served Jesus well; imagine how well they will serve us!

For reference, I've added several Scripture passages to these spiritual disciplines:

- **Fasting** (God's chosen fast, Isaiah 58:1–7; a partial fast, Daniel 10:1–14; a normal fast, Nehemiah 1:4–11; absolute fast, Esther 4:12–17)
- **Solitude** (prayer and solitude, Matthew 6:5–6 and Luke 5:16; the insights of solitude, Psalm 8; solitude of the garden, Matthew 26:36–46; solitude of the cross, Matthew 27:32–50)
- **Study** (the call to study, Proverbs 1:1–9, 23:12–23; the value of study, Luke 10:38–42)
- **Submission** (Psalm 143:10; Matthew 6:10, 12:50, 26:42; John 5:30; Acts 21:14; Hebrews 13:21; 1 John 2:17)
- **Simplicity** (Psalm 116:6; Matthew 18:2–3; Luke 18:17; 2 Corinthians 11:3)
- **Meditation** (the glory of meditation, Exodus 24:15–18)
- **Guidance** (the guidance of divine providence, Genesis 24:1–21)

Jesus had a robust prayer life. There is hardly anything Jesus did without praying first. The Gospel of Mark explains that at the beginning of his ministry, Jesus got up while it was still dark to a deserted place where he prayed. His disciples wondered where he was and went to look for him. They eventually found him, but not until after he had spent time with his Father (Mark 1:35–39).

It is noteworthy that Jesus got up early to pray, as the scripture says. Here again, he practiced solitude. In response to Simon and the other disciples, Jesus said he wanted to go into the neighboring towns to proclaim the message. He was dedicated to his mission and purpose. He submitted to God's will. How dedicated are we to our prayer lives? In the Gospels, Jesus prays on many occasions during his earthly ministry. If Jesus prayed so often, how is it that some ministers avoid prayer? What damage results from a weak prayer life?

A lot of religious leaders are so overly concerned with taking care of everyone else that they often neglect themselves. Where Jesus said, "Let us go on to the neighboring towns, so that I may proclaim the message there also" (Mark 1:38), these ministers might have been inclined to go back to those searching for Jesus, like the disciples suggested, to take care of them rather than moving on.

We should strive to emulate Jesus. Praying constantly, spending time in solitude, and meditating are all ways we proclaim the good news. In other words, present our bodies at the altar, or as Saint Francis of Assisi is believed to have said, "Preach the Gospel at all times, and if necessary use words."

Jesus was unapologetic about his decision to seek solitude to pray. "Then Jesus went with them to a place called Gethsemane; and he said to his disciples, 'Sit here while I go over there and pray'" (Matt. 26:36). This was likely the most stressful moment in Jesus's life, yet he spent time in solitude and prayer. Solitude gives us time to go on an inward journey where we can hear God through self-examination and meditation. Similarly, Jesus asked God to remove the cup, but he submitted to God's will, nonetheless. There is peace in submission. We can see that Jesus gained strength through the practice of spiritual disciplines, becoming obedient and radically submissive to the point of death on the cross.

A Special Note for Spiritual Leaders

God's desire for the high priests was not to be above the people but to be among the people. The writer of Hebrews explains that the high priest was "able to deal gently with the ignorant and wayward" (Heb. 5:2) because he was also human and sinful. It was because of their sinful human nature that the high priest "must offer sacrifice for his own sins as well as for those of the people" (Heb. 5:3). In the same way, there is a need for ministers and church leaders to realize that they too are subject to weakness; therefore, they need accountability partners. We must find a way to confess our sins. "If we confess our sins, he who is faithful and just will forgive us our sins and cleanse us from all unrighteousness" (1 John 1:9). If we do not confess our sins, we can become trapped in a cycle where our sins become compounded. Ministers also need accountability partners. How can we minister to others if we do not address our own struggles first? Ministers must practice what we preach. Although it is profoundly challenging, ministers must help the congregation appreciate honesty, transparency, and openness, even when it pertains to our own struggles. A perfect minister is a lying minister.

Here are ways ministers and leaders can confess:

- Develop a trustworthy circle within or outside the congregation. Identify accountability partners.
- Spouses are ideal accountability partners. Remember, the purpose of marriage is to get each other to heaven, so leverage that teammate!
- Confess to the congregation, and develop trust and credibility by doing so.
- Confess to God (e.g., "[Cain,] what have you done?" [Gen. 4:10]. That was Cain's opportunity to confess the awful thing he had done, but he chose to lie to God.)
- Set boundaries around family time, personal time, and devotional time.

- Seek counsel, even mental health therapy. Proverbs 12:15 says "the wise listen to advice." Galatians 6:2 instructs us to "bear one another's burdens." We should mentor one another. Still, there may be times when we need a trained therapist. Perhaps a real friend will suffice. Real friends tell us the truth, not necessarily what we want to hear.

Spiritual Disciplines

In addition to referencing the Scripture passages identified with the spiritual disciplines outlined previously in this chapter, knowledge of these disciplines, accompanied by brief descriptions, will help us grow in our faith journey.

Celebration

We need to celebrate God. Our faith practice should not be subtle and solemn all the time. Jesus says that "a city built on a hill cannot be hid" (Matt. 5:14). Well, that may sound a bit obnoxious, but it is not. It means we are to let our light shine. Like a lighthouse guiding ships at sea to shore, our light should shine brightly, guiding to Christ those lost in a sea of sin. It is okay to be excited about faith. There are many ways to celebrate faith: singing songs of joy to God like David did, taking a trip to the Holy Land and walking in Jesus's footsteps, writing devotionals or poems about faith, painting a portrait of a biblical scene, and shouting "amen" in church.

Exercise

"Train yourself in godliness, for, while physical training is of some value, godliness is valuable in every way, holding promise for both the present life and the life to come" (1 Tim. 4:7–8).

Scripture is not dismissing exercise but is setting godliness as supreme. In fact, this passage endorses physical exercise, taking care of ourselves, as a form of celebrating faith.

Rest

According to Genesis 1, God rested on the seventh day of creation. If God rested on the seventh day, why should I be so arrogant to think I do not need to rest? Refer to Chapter Six for a deep dive into the Sabbath rest principle.

Submission

Each of these spiritual disciplines requires the discipline of submission. In submission, we recognize the legitimate authority of others over us. It is nothing more than the simple understanding that "no man is an island." Life in community is our rightful home; relationships with other human beings are our inheritance. To confess our commitment to community means to confess our commitment to mutual subordination. Peter crystallized this principle in the simple phrase, "Honor everyone" (1 Pet. 2:17), and Paul set forth the idea in what must be considered the most memorable sentence on the subject: "Be subject to one another out of reverence for Christ" (Eph. 5:21).

This raises issues that are deep and difficult, such as submitting to the ways of God, to the state, to the Christian fellowship, to our Christian households, and much more. Be wary of fake submission. Submission does not mean we are doormats, getting walked upon. Submission does not mean we are to be people pleasers. Paul said we cannot be people pleasers and worship God at the same time. "Am I now trying to win the approval of human beings, or of God? Or am I trying to please people? If I were still trying to please people, I would not be a servant of Christ" (Gal. 1:10 NIV).

Being dependent upon others can also be fake submission. There's a difference between accepting charity and expecting charity. In other words, we are not to take advantage of the good will of others. We are called to serve, beginning with taking care of ourselves so that we can help others. There may be situations when we have to depend on others in our time of need, but we are not called to remain dependent. Similarly, we are not to manipulate others or succumb to the manipulative nature of others who seek to control us, leading from the second chair.

True submission is often doing things we do not want to do. That is submission because it is dying unto self.

Simplicity

Simplicity is openness, unselfconsciousness, naturalness. It is the opposite of subtlety, cunning, duplicity. Where simplicity abounds, words can be taken at face value: there is no hidden agenda. Yet, simplicity is not synonymous with "easy to understand." Jesus was not easy to understand. Nor was Paul, but both were characterized by simplicity of speech. Their intent was not to confuse or deceive but to clarify and illuminate.

Service

In his most famous teaching on service, Jesus concluded, "For even the Son of Man did not come to be served, but to serve, and to give his life as a ransom for many" (Mark 10:45 NIV). Our Lord's unique service of redemption through the cross is unrepeatable. However, we are called to serve through the many little deaths of going beyond self. Rather than obsess over having power, control, and prestige, Jesus wants his disciples to busy themselves with doing good. Christian leaders should look for opportunities to place the needs of others ahead of their own. Their service should come from sincere hearts (Col. 3:22) and never out of a sense of pretense.

Combining each of these spiritual disciplines allows us to grow into the likeness of Jesus. We become people who can offer blessings to the world and in whom the spirit of God can sing.

Notes

[1] "Clergy More Likely to Suffer from Depression, Anxiety," Duke Global Health Institute, August 28, 2013, https://globalhealth.duke.edu/news/clergy-more-likely-suffer-depression-anxiety-0.

[2] "Excerpt: A Rapid Decline in Pastoral Security," Barna, March 15, 2023, https://www.barna.com/research/pastoral-security-confidence/.

9

PRACTICAL KEYS TO MEDITATION

Many Christians think meditation is of no benefit to them, and that is unfortunate. Some think meditation is exclusive to Eastern religions, yet we see meditation in the Scriptures. Genesis 24:63 describes Isaac meditating in the field: "He went out to the field one evening to meditate, and as he looked up, he saw camels approaching" (NIV). In the book of Joshua, the Lord says, "This Book of the Law should not depart out of your mouth, but you should meditate on it day and night. . . . For then you will make your way prosperous, and then you will have good success" (Josh. 1:8 ESV).

This chapter is not an all-inclusive meditation guide, but it is a guide to practical methods of meditation that I have found most helpful in my life. First, consider three more Scripture passages that reference meditation:

> Blessed is the one who does not walk in step with the wicked or stand in the way that sinners take or sit in the company

of mockers, but whose delight is in the law of the Lord, and who meditates on his law day and night. (Psalm 1:1-2 NIV)

May my meditation be pleasing to him, as I rejoice in the Lord. (Psalm 104:34 NIV)

May these words of my mouth and this meditation of my heart be pleasing in your sight, Lord, my Rock and my Redeemer. (Psalm 19:14 NIV)

It is clear that those who are children of God, each of us, regardless of our denomination or tradition, can delight and benefit by spending time in meditation. The methods provided below can be seamlessly woven into our daily routines.

Lectio Divina

Although popularized by Catholics, this form of meditation involves reading Scripture and then meditating on it. There are five steps:

1. *Invocare* (invoke)—Invite the Holy Spirit's guidance while reading Scripture.
2. *Lectio* (read)—Choose a Scripture reading, several verses but not too many, and read them repeatedly. I like to read them seven times.
3. *Meditari* (meditate)—Sit quietly and reflect on the scripture for seven minutes.
4. *Orotieo* (pray)—Speak to God. Pray for an open heart and open mind and that God's will be done. This is a good time to thank God and to ask how to relate to and apply the Scripture reading.
5. *Contemplatio* (contemplate)—Spend a few moments in silence, listening with heart and mind to God's will, and then contemplate how to put God's Word into practice.

Meditation in Nature

Creation itself testifies about its creator. "Ever since the creation of the world, his invisible attributes of eternal power and divinity have been able to be understood and perceived in what he has made. As a result, [people] have no excuse" (Rom. 1:20 NABRE).

Sometimes, when I want to meditate, I will spend time in nature, as I described in Chapter Three. Whether hiking in the mountains, on trails, or along a lake, I find peace in nature and enjoy experiencing God's creation. To avoid distractions, I will try to make myself reasonably comfortable as I sit and focus on the elements before me. In a sitting position with my back straight, I am able to breathe deeply, which is an important aspect of meditation, quieting the heart, mind, and body so that I can focus on the spirit. For instance, if sitting along a stream, I will watch the pattern on the water's surface, caused by the wind. Then, I replicate that pattern with my breath as I reflect. In that space, I have found creative energy and inspiration from God. In those moments, God communicates to me.

Box Breathing

Box breathing is a popular de-stressing technique. The name is derived from the fact that a box has four sides, and the exercise involves counting to four while breathing and then repeating the exercise four times. It is also known as square breathing, and it is used to aid in relaxation, reduce blood pressure and anxiety, and even reduce symptoms of asthma. Most importantly, it is a form of meditation.

Find a way to be still and attentive, yet comfortable. Remove any accessories like rings and bracelets—anything that could be distracting. Then simply inhale for four seconds, hold for four seconds, exhale for four seconds, and repeat four times. The exercise brings mental clarity and reduces anxiety.

Many preachers do this prior to addressing their congregations. Yes, even the most seasoned public speakers get nervous. I am no longer ashamed to admit I get a little nervous before preaching, and I hope that I never lose that nervousness when I'm preaching the Word of God. Often, I'll do this exercise just before I am about to preach, right there in front of the congregation, and no one is the wiser.

4-7-8 Breathing

The technique of 4–7–8 breathing has all the physical, mental, and spiritual health benefits of box breathing, but the technique is slightly different. It involves three steps:

1. Positioning the tongue against the roof of the mouth with the tip touching the back of the front teeth, inhale through the nose for four counts.
2. Hold for a count of seven.
3. Exhale—for an evenly paced eight count—through the mouth, with lips slightly pursed around the tongue to make a whooshing sound.

Keeping the pace even, repeat the above steps four times.

Prayer Rug

Many times, we pray like a food server shouting requests to a short-order cook. "God, please let me get this car loan." "God, thank you for this food. Let's eat." "God, please help me pass this test." That is no way to speak to the sovereign ruler of all creation. We need to get in the habit of sitting at the king's feet. I bought a prayer rug and some religious artwork and placed them in a nook in my home. I go to that space to pray. It is important to get into a proper prayer posture; there are several:

- *Sitting*—1 Chronicles 17:16–27
- *Standing*—Nehemiah 9:5; Mark 11:25; Luke 18:13
- *Walking*—2 Kings 4:35
- *Bowing*—Exodus 34:8; Nehemiah 8:6; Psalm 72:11
- *Raising Hands*—2 Chronicles 6:12–13; Psalm 63:5; 1 Timothy 2:8
- *Kneeling*—1 Kings 8:54; Ezra 9:5; Luke 22:41; Acts 9:40
- *Lying Prostrate*—Joshua 7:6; Ezra 10:1; Matthew 26:39; Mark 14:35

The two postures I use most with my prayer rug are bowing and lying prostrate. Mostly, I bow. The best part of having a prayer rug is that I can roll it up and take it with me when I travel. It's always clean. No one walks on the prayer rug. Prayer does not have to stop simply because of travel. When I go to my prayer rug or the prayer corner in my home, I set a timer for an hour or thirty minutes. Committing to this prayer time is imperative, as is choosing a prayer posture. I will bow before the throne of God with my face on the ground. I talk to God for the first few minutes, and I then remain silent, listening. Most of my prayer time is spent listening.

People who have done this with me end up with tears in their eyes. I have done this alone and ended up with tears in my eyes many times. It is very powerful. It fills and restores faith.

Beads

I have a beaded bracelet and a beaded necklace. A lot of people cannot see these because they are under my shirt collar or hidden by my sleeve. If I find myself in a restless moment, if I find myself doing what the Scriptures say not to do—that is, worry—I will begin to count each bead in that moment. Nobody knows I am doing it. No one has to know I am feeling stress. I could be in the midst of an intense moment, and I will take one hand to my bracelet or necklace and begin to count as I breathe in and out in rhythm with the count. Sometimes, I wear two beaded bracelets, and I can hear the clicking sound as I move one bracelet against the other while counting. All the while, I align my breathing to the count in my head and the clicking sound. This is a calming exercise. I use this to center myself with the will of God.

Whether in our homes, in nature, in the office, traveling, about to speak to a crowd of a thousand or a group of ten, about to interview for a job or take an exam—whatever the situation—there is a practical and simple tool for meditation. Avoid procrastination and excuse making. It may seem counterintuitive, but even in the midst of busyness or stress, consciously carving time and space for meditation and prayer will clear our minds, reduce anxiety, and bring us closer to God. I highly recommend getting into this habit.

10

THE PRACTICE OF SIMPLICITY

Whether because of insecurity, covetousness, gluttony, or the impressions of others, we tend to complicate our lives. Many of us recognize this in ourselves, and at different points throughout our life we try to improve ourselves. New Year's is a perfect example. At the dawning of a new year, we tend to envision the possibilities of becoming the person we want to be. For most, that involves losing weight or ditching bad habits. Our desire to improve ourselves is good. We must be sure, however, that as we aim to make changes, we do not change who God wants us to be. We should not set goals based on insecurity, covetousness, gluttony, or the impressions of others.

> Again, you have heard that it was said to those of ancient times, "You shall not swear falsely, but carry out the vows you have made to the Lord." But I say to you, do not swear at all, either by heaven, for it is the throne of God, or by the earth, for it is his footstool, or by Jerusalem, for it is the city of the great King. And do not swear by your head, for you cannot

> make one hair white or black. Let your word be "Yes, Yes" or "No, No"; anything more than this comes from the evil one.
> (Matt. 5:33–37)

By choosing to live simply, by letting our "yes" mean "yes" and our "no" mean "no," we are not allowing low self-esteem, covetousness, gluttony, or the impressions of others to complicate our lives or to confuse us. Where there is simplicity, there is no hidden agenda. Simplicity does not mean easy to understand. Jesus practiced simplicity, yet he was not easy to understand, nor was Paul. Neither intended to be haughty, make themselves look smart, or get a lot of nice stuff. Rather, they wanted to clarify, enlighten, and illuminate while always glorifying God.

In his book *Celebration of Discipline*, author Richard Foster notes that there are three types of spiritual disciplines: outward, corporate, and inward. Regarding simplicity, an outward discipline, Foster writes, "Simplicity is freedom. Duplicity is bondage. Simplicity brings joy and balance. Duplicity brings anxiety and fear."[1]

Adele Calhoun writes, "Simplicity asks us to let go of the tangle of wants so we can receive the simple gifts of life that cannot be taken away."[2] Unfortunately, many people do not enjoy the simple gifts of life because they find themselves tangled in the complex entangling of sin. John in his epistle classifies sins of commission in three categories: the lust of the flesh, the lust of the eye, and the pride of life. These three categories disrupt individuals' inner peace and create three inner wars: the war of self, the war of things, and the war of other people.

War of Self

War of self has to do with our ego. The ego requires constant restraint. Our ego loves applause, attention, and constant affirmation. Ego is what gives us a sense of superiority. Because of ego, we often compare ourselves to others, and we judge others and how we measure up to them. The Bible encourages us to constantly examine ourselves and our motives. "Examine yourselves to see whether you are living in the faith. Test yourselves. Do you not realize that Jesus Christ is in you?—unless, indeed, you fail to meet the test!" (2 Cor. 13:5).

Sometimes, our ego is not fueled by pride but by a lack of faith in what God can do with us and our abilities. This is low self-esteem. Below is a series of questions that can help one determine if a war of self is going on internally.

- *Do I put on airs about my ability or skill set?*
- *When someone asks me if I have read a book, do I say yes when I know I haven't read it?*
- *When someone asks me if I know of a person or public figure, do I say yes when I really do not?*
- *Do I use fanciful words to obscure my real intentions or hide my true ability?*
- *Do I try to look like I am very religious to impress others?* For some, the question might be: *Do I try to look more vulgar than I am to gain credibility with others?*
- *Do I try to impress people with my achievements, education, or titles?*

This war of the self causes individuals to strive to look a certain way or to maintain a certain image, but that's like a prison of one's own making. Eventually, we might find ourselves afraid of violating the image we created for ourselves. We may discover we are like the Wizard of Oz, who created for those around him a larger-than-life persona, yet he was terrified that someone might go behind the curtain and see him for who he really was.

When we let our "yes" be our "yes" and our "no" be our "no," we are who God made us to be. We do not have to prove ourselves, make ourselves look like something we are not, or feign intelligence. We can simply be, abiding in the Lord. Oh, how liberating!

War of Things

The familiar saying "keeping up with the Joneses" essentially means one feels pressure to match the neighbors in material possessions, item for item. Why do we feel this pressure? It could be fear or shame that others will think less of us. It could be fear of missing out. It could be a false sense that acquiring material items will lead to happiness. Whatever the reason, this need to acquire stuff can become addictive. As such, it becomes binding and can weigh us down.

> Keep your lives free from the love of money, and be content with what you have; for he has said, "I will never leave you or forsake you." So we can say with confidence, "The Lord is my helper; I will not be afraid. What can anyone do to me?" (Heb. 13:5-6)

When I was in Eswatini, one of the poorest countries in the south of Africa, I needed to get some cash. I was fearful about making the trip to the bank because the high exchange rate would mean that I would be carrying a lot of Eswatini bills. I, projecting onto the people of this foreign country the disposition I carried in the United States, assumed I would be robbed. The folks I was with assured me I had nothing to worry about, but I did not believe them. I approached the ATM as I would any ATM back home, looking around, scoping the people nearby. When the cash was dispensed, I quickly stuffed it into my pockets. Because I was so certain that I would be mugged,

I briskly walked back toward our van, which seemed far away. After getting back inside the vehicle, I felt safe, and then I realized no one cared about me or my ATM visit. Interestingly enough, I learned that Eswatini is one of the most peaceful countries in the world, which was clearly not the case of the city I was currently living in back home in the United States.

Thinking about this experience later, I wondered what the differences were between one of the poorest countries in the world and the United States, which by and large has relative poverty but is still one of the richest countries in the world. The difference between absolute and relative poverty is that the former has specific fiscal outlines, while the latter is established in relation to the economic climate of a particular community. According to endPoverty, a person or household unable to meet minimum living requirements over an extended period can be defined as experiencing absolute poverty. Those experiencing relative poverty generally receive 50 percent less income than average, making their situation one of social exclusion, not fiscal exclusion. The researchers note that "relative poverty also changes over time. As the wealth of a society increases, so does the amount of resources and income, that society deems necessary for proper living conditions. Therefore, relative poverty works in relation to the society in question."[3]

I realized that the difference between Eswatini, one of the poorest countries in the world, and the United States, one of the wealthiest, is profound covetousness.

Coveting is one of the so-called seven deadliest sins. It is greed, and it is sinful because when we covet things, when we are covetous about stuff others have, we are failing to be grateful for what we have. Failing to be grateful is akin to snubbing God. Covetousness can lead us to oppress others. It can lead to harmful actions, too. Why were the people in this poor country not covetous toward me? Perhaps it simply was their culture or a lack of 24-7 media reminding them that they are the "have-nots" or that if they only purchased this or that product, they would be happier. Perhaps these people do not even consider themselves poor. They live simply, and they are some of the happiest people I've met.

The war of things will push us to rob ourselves of true happiness and will lead us to bring misery upon ourselves if we saddle ourselves with crushing debt just to keep up with the Joneses. The virtues of charity and justice are the antidote to the war of things.

Here are some reflective questions to determine if one suffers with the war of things:

- *Do I live within my means?*
- *Am I content with my age?*
- *Do I leave the store with what I intended to get, or do I leave with items that I bought on impulse?*
- *Do I buy things I cannot afford in order to impress others?*

When we can free ourselves from the war of things or coveting what others have, it is to live a life of simplicity. Being content is about simplicity, and simplicity is liberating.

War of Other People's Perspective

Many of us often wonder what others think about us. Some may obsess over this, bending over backward to please others just to ensure we are looked upon favorably. Doing so gives others power over us, which may lead us to do things that go against our nature. Trying to please a boss at work, a friend, a family member, or even a complete stranger could lead us to forsake our call to righteousness. We sometimes get so caught up in trying to look good that we fail to do good. Why? Why do we give up that control of ourselves, and not because of peer pressure, but because of self-imposed pressure?

The internal war of other people's perspectives has many Christians and believers ensnared in the thoughts and opinions of others, but when we set our hearts and minds to be concerned only with what God thinks of us, we are practicing simplicity. We no longer are worried about what the boss thinks, our family thinks, our friends think, or that person sitting across from us on the train thinks. We have to be concerned only with pleasing God. Practicing such simplicity is liberating. "It is dangerous to be concerned with what others think of you, but if you trust the LORD, you are safe" (Prov. 29:25 GNT).

Here are some questions to determine whether we suffer from the war of people's thoughts:

- *Do I shape every narrative to benefit myself?*
- *Do I respond to every less-than-favorable remark about me?*
- *Do I always have an excuse to defend my behavior even when I know I am wrong?*
- *Do I do my best without worrying if someone is watching?*
- *Do I demonstrate false humility when I receive compliments, or do I dismiss them?*

The desire to improve ourselves is good, as long as it is born of God's will, not ours, and not out of our desire to impress someone else. "See, this alone I found, that God made human beings straightforward, but they have devised many schemes" (Eccl. 7:29). With every self-improvement effort, let us strive to be genuine, authentic, and real. Let us practice simplicity by letting our "yes" be our "yes" and our "no" be our "no," not just in our words, but also in our deeds—our finances, our relationships with others, and our view of ourselves.

Practicing simplicity will help us become free from a world of confusion and complication. Remember, confusion is the work of Satan, and God is not the author of confusion. God loves order. Let's submit to God, and let's free ourselves of the war of self, the war of things, and the internal war of other people's perspectives.

Notes

[1] Richard Foster, *Celebration of Discipline: The Path to Spiritual Growth*, 3rd ed. (New York: HarperCollins, 1998), 79.

[2] Adele Calhoun, *Spiritual Disciplines Handbook: Practices That Transform Us* (Downers Grove, IL: InterVarsity Press, 2005), 75.

[3] "Relative vs. Absolute Poverty," endPoverty, March 2, 2023, https://endpoverty.org/relative-poverty-vs-absolute-poverty/.

A MESSAGE TO THE READER

I pray that reading this volume has been a blessing to you. The principles I have compiled in this book were gathered over the course of many years, and it brings me great joy to encapsulate them for the purpose of helping you in your journey to spiritual liberation. Each of us has the opportunity and choice to take the journey. If we place our trust in Christ and decide to follow him, we open ourselves to potential blessings we cannot fathom—blessings in our lives and in the lives of those around us. Not everyone will choose to engage in the inward revolution, but if you do, I assure you the journey is quite rewarding. Go in peace, beloved!

Pastor Lawrence W. Rodgers

ACKNOWLEDGMENTS

This book, a labor of love and spiritual exploration, could not have come into being without the invaluable contributions of many. I am deeply indebted to each one of them.

My profound gratitude extends to my wife, Bettae, whose unwavering support and understanding during the countless hours I spent writing and practicing spiritual disciplines were truly indispensable. Her patience and wisdom have been my steadfast anchors. To my children, who have consistently been sources of inspiration and encouragement as I delved deeper into my spiritual journey, you are indeed my guiding lights. And to my parents, who ignited in me the initial spark of curiosity to explore both within and all around me, instilling a lifelong pursuit of understanding and connection.

I owe a tremendous debt of gratitude to the esteemed faculty of the Howard University School of Divinity. Professors such as Dr. Alton Pollard III, Dr. Kenyatta Gilbert, Dr. Alice Bellis, Dr. Gay Byron, Dr. Frederick Ware, Dr. Michael Newheart,

Dr. Renee Harrison, Dr. Harold Dean Trulear, and Dr. Cain Hope Felder have profoundly influenced my journey inward. They have been instrumental in connecting me with spiritual ancestors like Howard Thurman. I am particularly grateful to Dr. Gilbert for his meditation guidance and for introducing me to the powerful meditative practices of Dorothy Ann Wright. Similarly, Dr. Pollard's practical application of spiritual disciplines has been transformative in my spiritual growth.

The 2016 Ethiopia trip with the Howard University School of Divinity delegation, and especially our time with Memeher Dr. Zebene Lemma, was a pivotal moment in my spiritual journey, opening my eyes to the depth of African-centered spiritual disciplines.

Special thanks to the congregations, particularly Westside Church of Christ and Second Baptist Church of Detroit, that have been incubators of inspiration for this volume. Moreover, the institutions of higher learning that nurtured the thoughts within these pages—Harding University, Howard University School of Divinity, Abilene Christian University, and the University of Michigan—deserve recognition.

My heartfelt thanks to Kari Barlow for her gentle encouragement not to abandon my writing journey, and to Lorraine for coaching me in finding my unique writing voice. I am also grateful to Jason Fikes and Leafwood Publishers for making my first publication experience so rewarding.

Inspirational figures like Howard Thurman, Richard Rohr, Barbara Holmes, Dallas Willard, Bishop Desmond Tutu, Leon Wright, Willie Wilson, Richard J. Foster, and Eric Wilson have deeply influenced my work, providing timeless insights through their teachings and writings.

Lastly, I am thankful to God for providing me with the experiences and the energy required to develop this volume.

ACKNOWLEDGMENTS

Balancing my roles as a member of the clergy, scholar, and community servant has uniquely shaped this book, infusing it with a blend of spiritual insight and social empathy.

Every word in this book has been touched by the spirit and wisdom of these incredible individuals and experiences. I am eternally grateful for their influence on my journey and this work.

ABOUT THE AUTHOR

Pastor Lawrence W. Rodgers is a spirit- and grace-filled clergy person who appreciates the spirit of God working in his life and the lives of God's people. He believes that the church must always walk in the footsteps of Christ, following his guidance and example. As a church leader, he tirelessly works on behalf of the mission and will of Christ.

Rodgers pastors the historic Second Baptist Church of Detroit congregation in Detroit, Michigan. Second Baptist is a congregation established in 1836 by a group of self-determined formerly enslaved and free African Americans. He is happily married to his wife, Bettae, who is a doctoral candidate in health sciences at the University of Bridgeport and holds a bachelor's degree in biochemistry and a master's degree in pharmaceutical science. Their three children are a source of blissful joy.

Rodgers is a graduate of Harding University, where he studied Bible and ministry. He graduated with honors, including the Most Outstanding Bible and Ministry Major. Rodgers is a 2017 graduate of the Howard University School of Divinity, where he earned the master's degree in divinity. He graduated at the top of his class and with the following honors: the Biblical Scholarship Award for excelling in biblical and theological studies, the Donald Barton Prize for most likely to succeed in pastoral leadership, and the Delores Carpenter Award for "exemplifying the highest levels of academic achievement and embodying the commitment to do justice, love mercy, and walk humbly with God." Rodgers's commitment to social justice and mental health moved him to pursue a master's in social work at the University of Michigan, graduating in 2024.

Pastor Rodgers currently serves as the chair of public relations for the board of the Council of Baptist Pastors of Detroit and Vicinity. He serves as a board member for Downtown Outreach, an organization committed to social justice and social compassion in the heart of Detroit. He also has served as a board member for the Detroit Urban League.

Rodgers regularly preaches, lectures, and teaches college and congregational classes. He has served as an adjunct instructor for Abilene Christian University. Rodgers is a consultant for the Carl Spain Center on Race Studies & Spiritual Action, directed by Dr. Jerry Taylor. He has more than ten years of experience in congregational leadership in the areas of mentoring, preaching, advising, church growth, administration, and strategic planning.

He also is a researcher, lecturer, and teacher. He has been published in *The Christian Century*, Patheos, *KineticsLive*, and the *Rhetoric, Race, and Religion* (R3) blog. Rodgers's work has also been featured in *The AFRO* newspaper and the *Baltimore Sun*.

Rodgers has published chapters and articles in several academic and popular books. His work has also appeared in *Reconciliation Reconsidered*, edited by Tanya Smith Brice. Most recently, he was featured in *Wisdom Commentary: Proverbs* by Alice O. Bellis.

Pastor Rodgers's international work focuses on the continent of Africa. He has taught courses on theology and decolonization in Eswatini and Ghana. He was also a member of the Howard University delegation to Ethiopia in 2016, which returned the ancient manuscript Tweed MS150 to the Ethiopian Orthodox Church.

Pastor Rodgers is an activist in several social justice efforts. He is a talented program manager who has fundraised, created, and led projects to serve the homeless community, survivors of human trafficking, adult literacy, and STEM programs for children in areas such as financial literacy, robotics, and coding. His passion for reentry citizens led him to become a certified trainer for Healing Communities USA under the leadership of Rev. Dr. Harold Dean Trulear. Furthermore, Rodgers's commitment to food security fuels his interest in gardening and in the establishment of church and community gardens. This passion is sustained and informed by his partnership with the Black Church Food Security Network, pioneered by Dr. Heber Brown, III.

Pastor Rodgers plans to continue to fulfill the ministerial vision that has been laid upon his heart. He intends to continue to encourage the church locally and broadly to realize its potential and heavenly call to be a refuge for the afflicted, broken, and the lost. He is an advocate both in word and in deed. Ultimately, Rodgers believes the church on Earth is a glimpse of the church in heaven: a beloved community.

www.ingramcontent.com/pod-product-compliance
Lightning Source LLC
Chambersburg PA
CBHW060607080526
44585CB00013B/723